Craftsmen of the Word

Craftsmen of the Word

THREE POETS OF
MODERN RUSSIA

GUMILYOV · AKHMATOVA · MANDELSTAM

. BY LEONID I. STRAKHOVSKY

GREENWOOD PRESS, PUBLISHERS
WESTPORT, CONNECTICUT

Copyright © 1949 by the President and Fellows
of Harvard College

Reprinted by permission
of Harvard University Press

First Greenwood Reprinting 1969

Library of Congress Catalogue Card Number 79-91774

SBN 8371-2784-X

PRINTED IN UNITED STATES OF AMERICA

PREFACE

Believing that one cannot understand the present without knowing the past, I offer this study of Acmeism and of the three leading Acmeist poets, in order not only to fill an existing gap in our knowledge of pre-revolutionary Russian literature, but also as a means to the understanding of much of contemporary Soviet poetry.

Throughout this work my approach has been that of a literary historian rather than a literary critic. All translations of poetry, unless otherwise indicated, are mine. I have used my own system of transliteration, but I hope that some day all transliterations will be abandoned (except for library use) and that references and quotations of Russian material will be printed in Cyrillic type.

I wish to acknowledge the permission of the estate of Samuel Hazzard Cross, late editor of *The American Slavic and East European Review*, to reprint the essays on Nicholas Gumilyov and Anna Akhmatova, appearing here in a revised and enlarged form, as well as the permission of Dimitri von Mohrenschild, editor of the *Russian Review*, to reprint the somewhat enlarged essay on Osip Mandelstam and my translation of Gumilyov's poem "The Trolley Car That Lost Its Way." I also want particularly to thank Mr. Gerald Shelley for his courteous permission to use his translations of some poems by Anna Akhmatova and Nicholas Gumilyov; Professor Gleb

Struve, who gave valuable criticism and made available to me a copy of Gumilyov's military record *(Posluzhnoi spisok);* and Mrs. Chase Duffy of the Editorial Department, Harvard University Press, for splendid coöperation and excellent work in the preparation of the text for the printer. To my wife go my thanks for valuable advice and the painstaking typing of the manuscript.

Watertown, Massachusetts   L. I. S.

CONTENTS

Craftsmen of the Word

INTRODUCTION

The importance of poetry in the development of Russian literature has often been overlooked, perhaps mainly because of a lack of adequate translations. Yet from the time of Pushkin to the present, more poetry has been written and more poetry widely read and discussed in Russia than in any other country. The appearance of a new work by a well-known poet was always hailed not merely as a literary but as a national event.

Such predilection in Russia for poetry, although a constant factor, reached at times extraordinary proportions. Two such peaks can be observed: at the beginning of the nineteenth century when Pushkin and his pleiad held sway and then again at the beginning of the twentieth century which witnessed a second Golden Age of Russian poetry. Started by the Symbolists as a reaction against so-called "civic" poetry, which predominated in the second part of the nineteenth century, this revival of poetry in the first two decades of our century marked a real literary renaissance. And in this revival, the school of Acmeism and the three leading Acmeist poets—Gumilyov, Akhmatova, and Mandelstam—played a dominant role in the second decade, particularly during the seven years which preceded the revolutions of 1917.[1]

"The year 1910 marks the crisis of Symbolism," wrote Alexander Blok. "In that year were manifested new movements, which adopted a hostile attitude both to Symbolism and to one another: Acmeism, Ego-Futurism, and the first beginnings of Futurism."[2] The previous year saw the extinction of the once influential Symbolist review, *Vesy* (The Scales), and two years later the Acmeists took over from the Symbolists the banner of leadership in Russian poetry when they founded the Guild of Poets. Because the Acmeists set forth as their goal in poetry a chiseled verse, a precision of images, an exactness of epithets, detachment, a rational approach to creation, and, above all, craftsmanship and the proper use of the word in its exact and not its transitory meaning, they brought to Russian poetry a clarity and vigor which it had not known since the times of Pushkin. Hence they not only became the vanguard in the twentieth-century revival of poetry and were more read than other contemporary poets, but they laid down a permanent canon for the further development of Russian poetry.

"The Acmeists considered as their principal aim," wrote the critic Eikhenbaum, "the preservation of the verse as such; and the balance of all its elements—rhythmic as well as of meaning—was their principal concern. They refused to adopt the musical-acoustic point of view, but they preserved and improved the traditional rhythmic base."[3]

Although the Acmeist poets and their poetry are banned today in Soviet Russia because they were apolitical in their poetry, while Soviet literature in the credo of Lenin "cannot be apolitical,"[4] their influence on the development of some of the best contemporary Soviet poets is undeniable. "The influence of idealistic theories and of aesthetics is much stronger in poetry than in prose," says a recent editorial in the official organ of the Union of Soviet Writers. "Hence many outstanding Soviet poets, who began their creative careers before the revolution or shortly after it, were in direct creative contact with the representatives of Symbolism and Acmeism."[5] Of these the best known are Eduard Bagritsky, who died in 1934, Nikolai Tikhonov, Ilya Selvinsky, and Vissarion Sayanov, each of whom had acknowledged at one time or another his indebtedness to Acmeism.

When reviewing Sayanov's long poem "The Golden Olyokma," the Soviet critic Innokenty Oksyonov wrote: "The Acmeism of this remarkable poem lies in its extraordinary preciseness, clarity, and simplicity as well as in the combination of a manly lyrical intonation with a multitude of concrete details of the visible world."[6] Oksyonov also devoted a whole article to a revaluation of Acmeism under the title "Soviet Poetry and the Patrimony of Acmeism."[7] This was echoed by another Soviet critic, Nikolai Stepanov, who wrote in an article entitled "The Poetical Patrimony of Acmeism"[8] that the principles of Acmeism had gained of late a particularly important meaning and that the Acmeist treatment of verse was beginning to drive out the futuristic approach.

The reappearance of the poetry of Anna Akhmatova, the leading living Acmeist poet, under Soviet imprint and in leading Soviet periodicals between the years 1940 and 1946 was symptomatic of the general trend of acknowledging the Acmeist influence on the development of contemporary Russian poetry. But this trend was short lived, as it did not fit the policies of the leaders of Soviet Russia. They did nothing serious about it, however, during the war years, but on August 14, 1946, the axe fell when, by a resolution of the Central Committee of the Communist Party, the poetry of Anna Akhmatova was denounced and banned and the political nature of Soviet literature was once more reaffirmed.

NICHOLAS GUMILYOV

The Poet-Warrior

Nikolai Stepanovich Gumilyov, with his pale face, small black moustache, slightly slanting eyes, and drooping eyelids, with a frail body but a will of steel, might have been, if he had happened to be born in a different age, a Moses, a Mohammed, or a St. Ignatius Loyola. But he was born at the end of the "stupid nineteenth century" on April 15, 1886,[1] in Kronstadt, Russia, the son of a naval doctor, and he was a "poet by the grace of God"—a militant, fighting poet, a crusader about whom another poet said, "You never once in life took off your armor."[2]

Gumilyov's place in Russian literature as a poet, as a writer of prose "excellent in its formal perfection,"[3] as a critic who "felt the meaning of his epoch,"[4] as the acknowledged leader and master of a new literary school—Acmeism—has not yet been evaluated. His tragic death at the hands of a firing squad, when he was shot as a counter-revolutionary connected with the famous Tagantsev conspiracy, precludes any detailed study about him from appearing in the Soviet Union. And what has been written about him there so far, though recognizing Gumilyov's talent as a poet, is naturally tinged with Marxist bias. Almost nothing has been written about him abroad. Yet when writing his obituary, Peter Struve, who as editor of *Russkaya Mysl'* (The Russian Thought) had published both Gumilyov's

7

poetry and prose, expressed the opinion that "his poems will be included in all anthologies of Russian poetry."[5]

Having known Gumilyov personally and having belonged as a writer of poetry to his school, I offer this study as a tribute to his memory and as a small contribution to our better knowledge of that era of Russia letters between 1905 and 1917, which was a marked "renaissance" and to which Gumilyov so nobly contributed.

When I first met Gumilyov he was thirty, but looked older than his years. The first impression was that of restrained power. His manner was quiet, almost shy, but one could feel the inner strength, the unbounded courage of a fighter. Yet there was something very human, very tender about the man. He seldom laughed, but when he did it was the joyous laughter of a child. He loved life passionately, fundamentally. That is why, perhaps, he preferred the company of people younger than himself.

Serious though he appeared to be, he was not averse to youthful pranks or to spontaneous outbursts of gaiety. When we apprentices gathered at his studio-apartment we could never tell how the evening would end. It might be spent entirely in readings and discussions of poetry or it might be broken up for a game of tag or for a trip to see the gypsies in Novaya Derevnya. Or, as on one occasion that I recall, it might end in a surprise visit to some friends in Tsarskoye Selo when, after gathering a few bottles of champagne, we proceeded to the station, then rode in the train, and finally, piling into two sleighs, glided noiselessly through the quiet snow-covered streets of the tsar's residence. All the while (and before a bottle of wine had been opened) we were intoxicated by Gumilyov's presence, by his quiet yet sparkling conversation, by his good-humored sarcasm and brilliant repartee.

Such is the Gumilyov I recall—the man and the poet. As a man he may be forgotten by many, but as a poet he will live forever.

Russian poetry has two fundamental traditions stemming from its two central figures. Every Russian poet is bound by memories either of Pushkin or Lermontov, and it is interesting to note that everything of importance in Russian poetry is the result of a blend of these two traditions: one masculine— that of Pushkin, one feminine—that of Lermontov. No pure note has sounded yet, but as a general rule Lermontov's influence has prevailed. This could be explained by the fact that Russian poetry is still very young and, as the mother's influence is always stronger in childhood, so the feminine muse of Lermontov has held so far most of the Russian poets under its spell. One listens to the father's voice later, when life demands sustained force and manliness. "N. Gumilyov was the first representative of the manly tradition in our time. The blood ties with Pushkin and through him with classicism have not been felt so clearly in any of Russia's contemporary poets as in Gumilyov, whose poetry is a firm and decisive step on this new road. If among our contemporaries there have been poets more enchanting than he, still N. Gumilyov represents the most important figure in Russian poetry of the first quarter of the twentieth century, because he not only gave us examples of unsurpassed mastery, but also revealed to Russian poetry her destiny and the ways to reach it."[6]

Gumilyov started writing verse at the age of eight, and even before that he composed fables. His childhood was spent in Tsarskoye Selo (now Pushkin), but in 1895 his family moved to St. Petersburg (now Leningrad) where Gumilyov began his studies in the private school of Gurevich. In 1900 the family left St. Petersburg and settled in Tiflis (now Tbilisi) in the Caucasus where Gumilyov attended the public schools. At this time he became interested in Marxian socialism and even carried on socialist propaganda among a group of flour-mill workers. In 1903 the family returned to Tsarskoye Selo and Gumilyov entered the Nicholas Gymnasium, the principal of which was the poet Innokenty Annensky. Under his influence Gumilyov finally came to realize that his calling was poetry and henceforth devoted his energies to the pursuit of success in his chosen field. His early interests in socialist ideas were replaced by a complete devotion to the art of poetry and by an antipathy for politics.[7]

During Gumilyov's formative years, while he was still at school, the Russian literary scene was monopolized by the Symbolists. There was something Germanic, misty, unreal, and amorphous in the art of the Symbolists. To this Gumilyov opposed the clarity, the sunniness, the precision of the Gallic spirit. While the Symbolists faithfully followed Verlaine's recipe "de la musique avant toute chose" and "pas la couleur, rien que la nuance," Gumilyov looked for his model and guide in Théophile Gautier's famous pronouncement: "L'art robuste seul a l'éternité." Nevertheless, Gumilyov started his career as a poet in the ranks of the Symbolists whose importance in the development of Russian letters he had never denied and whose contribution he characterized as follows: "Russian Symbolists had set for themselves a difficult but lofty task—to bring our native poetry out of a Babylonian captivity formed by petty ideals and prejudice, a captivity in which it had lingered for almost half a century."[8] "Symbolism is the result of maturity of the human spirit when that spirit proclaimed that the world is what our conception of it is." And he added: "But at present we cannot be Symbolists. This is not an appeal, not a wish, but merely a certified fact."[9]

Yet from the beginning Gumilyov's poetry had elements

in it which clearly indicated that his sojourn among the Symbolists was merely a temporary one and that soon he was to find a different way, his own. "The impressionistic attachment to music of the Symbolists was contrasted by Gumilyov with the painter's quality and plasticity of images; the subjective lyricism with a severe epic form; the foggy stream of words made half-articulate in their meaning with 'a conscious and rational word-use.'"[10] Already in his first book, entitled characteristically, *Put' Konkvistadorov* (The Way of the Conquistadors), he showed his predilection for color, and bright color at that, for the sunny beauty of southern climes, and for the romance and adventure of exploring little-known exotic lands. In this he emulated Valery Bryusov, "but this tendency toward the exotic together with the romantic fantasies proved with him to be of a more realistic nature."[11]

In these still immature poems, such as the following, one can see already the fundamental difference between the romanticism of the early Symbolists and the romanticism of Gumilyov.

> With you I will remain till dawn,
> But on the morrow go
> To look for the retreat of kings
> Who have embraced the star.
>
> . . .
>
> Their swords, weighed down with precious stones,
> Around them idly lie,
> While gnomes keep careful watch on them,
> And will not leave their post.
> But with my sword I shall be there,
> 'Tis not a gnome that owns it!
> And I shall be the thunderstorm,
> The lightning and the fire.
>
> . . .

With you I'll greet again the dawn,
But on the morrow go,
And give you for my last farewell
The star which I have won.[12]

As can be seen, Gumilyov has a different motive from the
Symbolists for roaming in a fantastic, unreal world. It is not
disenchantment with real life that leads him into a romantic
realm, but the desire to win "the star" by the force of his own
sword. This theme is developed even more pointedly in the
sonnet which opens the book.

Conquistador in iron armor,
Pursuing gaily my own star;
I walk o'er precipice, through canyon,
And only rest in joyful lands.

The fog grows grim in starless skies,
But I am silent and I wait;
And I have faith—I'll find my love,
Conquistador in iron armor.

If stars can hear no sunlit words,
I shall create my own bright dream;
And charm it with the songs of battle.

A brother I to storm and chasm;
But to my battle dress I add
The star of fields—a fleur de lis.[13]

This book was written while Gumilyov was in his last year
at school in Tsarskoye Selo and showed the author's imma-
turity as a poet. In a review of the book Valery Bryusov, who
was to become Gumilyov's much admired master and model,
criticized the young author severely, pointing out also that

Gumilyov was far from perfect in form, style, and verse. This was a challenge, and Gumilyov accepted it to work painstakingly on perfecting his technique and to emerge later as an unchallengeable master of form, style, and verse, as if the precept of Theophile Gautier "l'oeuvre sort plus belle d'une forme au travail rebelle, vers, marbre, onyx, émail," which was to become his canon, was already his guiding star. But Bryusov recognized the talent of the young poet when he closed his review with the words: "But the book has also some very beautiful poems, some very effective images. Let us hope that it is only the way of a new conquistador, whose victories and conquests lie still ahead."[14] Notwithstanding Bryusov's criticism (or perhaps because of it), the Symbolist review *Vesy* (The Scales) opened its pages to the new author. From 1906 to 1909 *Vesy* published thirteen poems and four short stories by Gumilyov.

In 1906, after completing his secondary education, Gumilyov went to Paris where he attended the Sorbonne, studying painting, French literature, and the Old French language. In Paris Gumilyov published a Russian literary magazine *Sirius*, in which the first verse of Anna Akhmatova appeared in print.[15] During his stay abroad he undertook a two months' trip to Egypt and the Sudan in the autumn of 1907, which marked the beginning of his interest in Africa. It was also in Paris that his second book of verse *Romanticheskie Tsvety* (Romantic Flowers) was published in 1908. In it one can already feel the influence of the Parnassians—Leconte de Lille, Hérédia, and Henri de Regnier—which was to become stronger in later years, although Gumilyov's poetic world is still peopled by romantic images. "Here through a symbolist pattern the true face of Gumilyov is already apparent."[16] His favorite themes still deal with knights in armor, with conquistadors, conquerors, emperors, majestic heroes, the Devil, Satan, Lucifer, the Serpent, the Raven, the Eternal Jew, Ossian, Sindbad the Sailor, Caracalla. They all perform great deeds as a prototype of Gumilyov's own ideal. But side by side there appear some poems of somber wisdom.

The Founders

Romulus and Remus went up the hill.
The hill was mute and bare before them.
Romulus said: "We'll build a town here."
"A town like sunshine," Remus replied.
Romulus said: "The stars have willed it,
And we have regained our ancient honor."
Remus replied: "What was before
We must forget, let us look forward."
"Here'll be a circus," Romulus said,
"Here'll be our house open to all."
"But we should put closer to our dwelling
The burial vaults," Remus replied.

It would be an error to think of the early Gumilyov, "who loved life passionately,"[17] always as a romantic, sunny poet. He had his somber moods. But even in his darkest moments he never forgot the force and power of man's will:

The Choice

The builder of towers will lose his grip,
And his fall through space will be frightful.
At the bottom of the well of the world
He will curse his own madness.

The one who destroys will be crushed.
Will be broken by slabs of stone;
And, abandoned by All-Seeing God,
Will yell in his utter despair.

And the one who retires to the caves,
Or the banks of the peaceful stream,
Will encounter the frightful stare
Of the awe-inspiring black panther.

None will escape the bloody fate
That to men has been allotted.
But wait: our incomparable right
Is to choose the death that we will.

Romanticheskie Tsvety reflects also Gumilyov's exoticism which had been revealed in his first book and was now enhanced by personal experience. The result of his trip to Africa can be seen in such poems as "Lake Chad," "Rhinoceros," "Jaguar," "Hyena," and "Giraffe." A line from the latter, which reads "Far, far away, by Lake Chad there wanders a *dainty** giraffe," was very much commented upon at the time of the appearance of *Romanticheskie Tsvety*, because people could not imagine a giraffe to be dainty and thought the epithet somewhat *recherché*.

In 1908 Gumilyov returned to Russia and settled in Tsarskoye Selo. Here he struck up a friendship with his former school principal, Innokenty Annensky, and later with the dean of the St. Petersburg Symbolists, Vyacheslav Ivanov, under whose leadership, but upon Gumilyov's initiative, a group named *Akademiya Stikha* (The Academy of Verse) was organized. This was the nucleus of *Obshchestvo Revnitelei Khudozhestvennogo Slova* (The Society of Adepts of the Artistic Word) which in 1913 counted fifty-seven members, mostly poets.[18] In 1909 he participated in the organization of the artistic review *Apollon*, the first issue of which appeared in October of that year. It is around this review and the Society of

---

*Italics supplied *(izyskanny)*.

Adepts of the Artistic Word that Gumilyov's talent as a poet and critic developed in the ensuing seven years. Although he published his poems in other reviews as well, particularly in *Russkaya Mysl'*, it was on the pages of *Apollon* that most of his important poems did appear, such as "The Captains," published in the first issue, and "The Discovery of America," published in December 1910.

Writing in the second issue of *Apollon*, Innokenty Annensky, one of the most sensitive poets of the period, had this to say about Gumilyov as a poet: "It seems that Nicholas Gumilyov feels color more than contour, and loves the dainty more than the musically beautiful. He works a great deal over the material of his poems and at times reaches an almost French exactness. His rhythms are elegantly alarming . . . Gumilyov's lyricism is an exotic longing for the colorfully picturesque patterns of the distant south. He loves everything that is peculiar and strange, yet his true taste makes him severe in the choice of his settings."[19] But it was as a critic and theorist of verse as well as the leader of the Acmeist school of poetry that Gumilyov emerges in his true stature from the pages of *Apollon*.

Beginning with the second issue of *Apollon* in November 1909, Gumilyov published regularly his *Pis'ma o russkoi poezii* (Letters about Russian Poetry). When reviewing these collected critical essays, published after the poet's untimely death, Bryusov, who had accepted the Bolshevik revolution, remarked: "This book by N. Gumilyov deserves attention primarily because the author emerges victorious from a difficult assignment . . . Gumilyov had the feeling of a genuine critic; his evaluations are to the point; they express in brief formulas the very essence of the poet . . . It is an interesting and valuable book. True, it is impressionistic criticism. True, it is poetry cut off from all currents of social life. True, it is the judgment of our entire literature by an Acmeist not devoid of bias. But it is a book of a poet who loved and understood art . . . Literary historians and historians of our own social development will still have to refer to this book by N. Gumilyov."[20] One cannot but agree unreservedly with Bryusov's evaluation of Gumilyov as a critic.

Gumilyov had a high concept of the calling of a poet "who must have his own word to say, no matter at what cost, which alone *makes* a poet." To him "simplicity and unpretentiousness of plot frees the word, makes it supple and sure, permits it to shine with its own light." And he exclaims: "How often people mistake for poetical talent an affluence of thoughts, a richness and a variety of impressions! It is precisely these qualities which prevent a person lacking poetical talent from becoming even a fair versifier." He admits that "from times immemorial prophets have put in verse their revelations, moralists their laws, philosophers their mental conclusions. It is a characteristic fact that nearly all insane people begin to write verse. Every valuable or simply peculiar aspect of an outlook on life strives to be expressed in verse . . . But, of course, such striving in most cases has no relation whatsoever to poetry." Why then do poets write? "This question is not difficult to answer: On one hand, to tell people something new, gained by themselves alone—an idea, an image, a feeling, it makes no difference; on the other hand, for the sheer ecstasy of creation, so divinely complicated, so joyfully difficult." And about those who claim that it has become easy to write poetry, he remarks: "They are partly right. We are indeed living through a poetical renaissance. Special attention is paid to poetry; it is considered fashionable to be interested in it, and no wonder that more and more poetry is being published . . . But to write good poetry is as difficult now as ever."[21]

At the time when aestheticism was making a bid to dominate Russian literature, he wrote: "The fault of the aesthetes lies in that they are seeking the foundation for their elegant admiration in the object and not in the subject. Terror, pain, disgrace are beautiful and endearing because they are bound so unbreakably with the whole universe and with our creative domination of everything. When one loves life like a mistress, one does not differentiate in the moment of caresses where pain ends and joy begins; all that one knows is that one wants nothing different." And he adds: "In not too cultured circles it is the custom to regard utter prettiness as a mark of aestheticism. But then it is the same as to call a 'gourmet' a person who eats sugar by the spoonful." To this he opposes what he believes to be the proper way of dealing with beauty, when he says: "An Acmeist represents not the beautiful, but his feeling of it."[22] And to the purists he throws this challenge: "Purity is suppressed sensuality and it is beautiful; but a complete lack of sensuality shocks one like a new unheard-of form of debauchery."[23]

To Gumilyov, the young poets of his time were "seafarers who like Sindbad leave behind their blessed Bagdad in order 'to gaze with curiosity at new things.' And their saving grace is only their reverent attitude toward the greatest possession of poets—their native language, as Sindbad's saving grace was his reverence for the laws of Allah." According to him, "only by severe work, by a constant effort, talent acquires variety without which there is no great creation." And he laments: "How sad it is to see a real poet seeking his way carefully and painstakingly, regretting to abandon what has already been discovered and refusing to acquire the saving dizziness of conquerors."[24]

Gumilyov was a perfectionist. To him Pushkin was the greatest manifestation of Russian poetic genius and the unques-

tionable proof of autochthonic Russian culture. When reviewing Alexander Blok's poems he wrote: "Usually a poet gives
to his readers his works. Blok gives himself. By this I mean that
in his poems one finds not only no solution, but not even any
indication of some general problem—a literary one as with
Pushkin, philosophic as with Tyutchev, or sociological as with
Hugo. He simply describes his own life, which luckily for him
is so astonishingly rich in internal struggle, catastrophes, and
illuminations . . . He has the particular Pushkin capacity to
make one feel the eternal in the merely passing, to show behind every occasional image the shadow of genius which is
guiding his fate."[25]

Russian culture to Gumilyov was neither of the West nor
of the East, but an entity of its own. "The most sensitive for-
eigners are convinced," he wrote, "that Russians are quite a
separate, a strange people. The mysteries of the Slavic soul—
l'âme slave—are a commonplace in the West. But they are content in describing its contradictions. However, we Russians
ought to go further and seek the sources of these contradictions. Undoubtedly we are not only a transition from the psychology of the East to the psychology of the West, or vice
versa, but we are already a whole and complete organism,
proof of which is Pushkin. But among us there happen to be,
as a general rule, throwbacks to the essence of one or the other
of the component parts. Thus Bryusov is a European completely and always, in every line of his poetry, in every word
even of the most insignificant of his articles . . . But Vyacheslav Ivanov is from the East . . . And in defending the wholeness of the Russian idea, we must stubbornly decry this extreme, even though loving it, and remember that it is not an ac-
cident that the heart of Russia is simple Moscow and not the
resplendent Samarkand."[26]

Such were Gumilyov's principal conceptions as a critic. But above all he was a poet who demanded much of others because he demanded much of himself. Poetry to him was the *acme* of human expression. That "verse is the highest form of speech, everyone knows who, while attentively chiseling a piece of prose, has had to use effort in order to prevent the bursting of nascent rhythm."[27] And "in verse the rhyme is the same as an angle in plastic art: it is a transition from one line to another and as such must be outwardly unexpected, inwardly well founded, free, tender, and elastic." According to him "poetry must hypnotize—in this lies its force" and "one of the unquestioned characteristics of good poetry is that it can be easily remembered."[28]

As to form, Gumilyov has explored almost all the existing ones from the sonnet, probably the most perfect form created in the West, to the Persian ghazali of the East. While reviewing a book of sonnets he said this about them: "A love for sonnets usually flares up either in an era of poetical renaissance or, on the other hand, in an era of decline of poetry. In the first case in the tight form of the sonnet are found new possibilties—either the meter is being varied or the sequence of rhymes is being changed; in the second case, the most complicated and unyielding, yet at the same time the most typical, form of the sonnet is being sought and it attains the characteristics of a canon. Shakespeare's sonnets and the sonnets of Hérédia are the two poles in the history of the sonnet and both of them are perfect. The difference in their methods permits one especially to appreciate their charm based, as always in sonnets, exclusively on an inspired calculation. In the former as in the latter the refinement of effect goes hand in hand with a sureness of expression and a rigidity of style."[29]

As a poet, Gumilyov gives his own formula for what constitutes a perfect poem. In a remarkable article entitled "Zhizn' stikha" (Life of the Verse) he wrote:

A poem must have thought and feeling, as without the first a lyric poem will be dead and without the second even an epic ballad will seem to be a boring unreality; it must have the softness of contour of a young body where nothing protrudes and nothing is lost, and the sharpness of a statue illuminated by the sun; it must have simplicity, because the future is open to it alone, and refinement as a living avowal of the heritage of all the joys and sorrows of past ages; and above all this—it must have style and gesture.

In style God shows himself through his own creation; the poet reveals himself, but a hidden self unknown even to himself, permitting one to guess the color of his eyes, the shape of his hands. . . By gesture in a poem I understand such a placement of words, such a choice of vowels and consonants, of speeding up and of slowing down of rhythm, that the reader of the poem involuntarily adopts the pose of his hero, repeats his facial expressions and his body movements and thus, thanks to this imaginary transformation of his own body, feels the same things as the poet himself so that the thought expressed from a lie becomes the truth. . .

A poem possessing the enumerated qualities, in order to be worthy of its name, must retain among them complete harmony and, what is most important, must have been evoked to life not "by the irritation of a captive thought," but by an internal necessity which gives it a living soul—temperament. Besides, it must be perfect even to its faults. . . In one word, a poem must be a cast, a likeness of the beautiful human body, this highest form of imaginable perfection. After all, men have created even God himself according to their own image and likeness.[30]

In the winter of 1909-10 Gumilyov interrupted his literary work for a six-months' trip to Abyssinia. Soon after his return to Russia in the spring of 1910 he married the poetess Anna

Akhmatova and spent his honeymoon in Paris. In that year also appeared his third book of poetry *Zhemchuga* (Pearls), dedicated to "my teacher—Valery Bryusov." In a review of this book Vyacheslav Ivanov wrote: "A master has no need for an imitator—he rejoices in an apprentice. A great master demands that a true apprentice have an independent talent and then on such a talent he imposes obedience, because in free obedience force matures. It is not out of place then when N. Gumilyov calls Valery Bryusov his teacher, because he is a pupil whom the master cannot fail to recognize."[31] Indeed Gumilyov was a pupil according to his own formula: "A real pupil always comes to the teacher with his own substance and in his outer submission there can always be discerned the challenge of future liberation."[32]

Many of the poems in *Zhemchuga* had previously appeared in *Vesy, Russkaya Mysl'* and *Apollon* and some, including "The Founders" and "The Choice," were reprinted from *Romanticheskie Tsvety*. The book contains also such poems as "The Witch," "The Old Conquistador," and "The Knight with a Chain," which are reminiscent of Gumilyov's earlier work, but the general character of the book is that of transition from romanticism to his new concept of Acmeism. Gumilyov is still an apprentice not only of Bryusov but of his own muse; but unlike Bryusov, who adhered to the formula "art for art's sake," Gumilyov believed in "art for life's sake."[33] He is still seeking his way, but one can already discern what it is in such remarkable long poems as "The Dream of Adam" and "The Captains." The romantic tendency is still strong but the images become more realistic, as when he says:

> The moon sails like the round shield
> Of a hero slain long, long ago.

He still likes color, but he is already showing his worship of the word—the precise, sharp, powerful, magic, miraculous, divine word, which raises the human being from his animal surroundings and makes him man. He has not yet mastered the word but he has discovered it. To him it appears still as somewhat lost in man's daily surroundings:

> The word is being born in pain and torture
> And quietly it goes through life, the timid one.

This is a far cry from what Gumilyov will have to say about the word in later years, but he is already preoccupied with defining its right place and its sober meaning. *Zhemchuga* shows that he was on the road to becoming "a great master in the field of the artistic word."[34]

In the autumn of 1911 Gumilyov and Sergei Gorodetsky founded a literary group called *Tsekh Poetov* (The Guild of Poets)[35] which was to become the nucleus of the Acmeist movement. The following spring he visited Italy and in the autumn of that year entered the University of St. Petersburg for the purpose of studying Old French poetry. It was also in 1912 that Gumilyov's fourth book of poetry, *Chuzhoe Nebo* (Foreign Skies), was published.

Among the poems in this new book were included five Abyssinian songs which according to Bryusov revealed "brilliant coloring and a great mastery."[36] Of the whole book Bryusov wrote: "There is a certain movement forward in the new collection of poems *Chuzhoe Nebo* by N. Gumilyov. Cold as before, but always well thought through, Gumilyov's poems leave an impression of the work of a talented artist, who loves his art and who is familiar with all the mysteries of poetic technique. Gumilyov is no teacher, no preacher; the importance of his poetry lies more in *how* he says it rather than in *what* he says. One has to love the very verse, the very art of the word for itself in order to love Gumilyov's poems . . . Gumilyov writes and will continue to write beautiful poetry."[37]

So Gumilyov—the conquistador and the apprentice—had traveled a long way since the appearance of his first book to receive recognition from his master as a new master of the craft, although *Chuzhoe Nebo* does not represent the peak of Gumilyov's growth as a poet.

The most outstanding poetical work in this book is a long poem entitled "The Discovery of America" (first published in *Apollon*), almost a companion piece to his previous "The Captains," but revealing a greater depth of thought and a much greater technical mastery. In this poem "every stanza is composed of six lines with two rhymes and the fourteen stanzas composing each song exhaust all possible combinations of two rhymes in six lines."[38]

In one of the best poems of this book, "Generals of the Turkestan Campaign," Gumilyov tells how strange it is to see these veterans at dances and receptions standing by the wall, polite and worldly, as if they had forgotten the days of anxiety, the nightly calls "To arms!" the lonely desert, the steady tread of camels' feet, the loss of friends and comrades, and the Russian flag waving over white Khiva.

> Forgotten? No! When every hour,
> Some minor instance, a mere trifle,
> Befogs the sparkle of their quiet eyes,
> Tells them of what has been before.
>
> "What is it?"—"Nothing, just the foot hurts."
> "Gout?"—"No, a bullet wound right through."
> And so the heart is promptly longing
> To be in sunny Turkestan.

This poem, together with some later ones about Africa, has been compared by Soviet critics with similar ones of Kipling, "the bard of English imperialism."[39] True, there is something of Kipling in certain of Gumilyov's poetry, but it is not in form or inspiration, but rather in feeling. Like Kipling, Gumilyov was somewhat of a "colonial" and it was not in jest (as some people thought at the time) that he advocated for Russia extension of her dominion over Abyssinia, a country supposedly professing the same type of Christianity. "Attracted by the war-like qualities of Russian imperialism, Gumilyov sought to create a poetry characterized by both rationalism and will. Thus he came to found the movement of Acmeism, headed by himself."[40]

It was also in 1912 that the Guild of Poets started the publication of the magazine *Hyperboreos* which was devoted entirely to the production of the poetry of this group.[41] The group was composed of the following: Gumilyov, Sergei Gorodetsky, Anna Akhmatova, Osip Mandelstam, Vladimir Narbut, Mikhail Zenkevich, and Georgi Ivanov. Of these Gumilyov, Akhmatova, and Mandelstam were outstanding. They actually formed the nucleus of the Acmeist movement, which later embraced a much larger number of the younger poets of Russia. When writing about this group in later years, a contemporary critic remarked: "If, on one hand, the Symbolists were blind (at that only a few of them could so *listen* to the world as did Blok!), then, on the other, the Acmeists were endowed with an extraordinary poetical vision. Like Adam in Gumilyov's poem, they seemed to see the world for the first time and looked at it with eyes which had not yet lost their primeval sharpness; like Adam they were glad to give a name to everything they saw."[42]

And Gumilyov was not only the theorist of the group, but

its unchallenged head. "Self-reliant, energetic, straightforward, not at all a dreamer, with a clear and direct mind, he felt himself different from the Symbolist poets. Having firmly and calmly analyzed the literary tendencies of his time, Gumilyov planned for himself with a cold deliberation his own poetical road." He was also different from the other members of the Acmeist group primarily because of "his active, honest, and simple manliness, his intense spiritual energy, and his temperament."[43]

The Acmeist group of poets received quick recognition, not only because they struck a different note, but principally because they wrote good poetry. Years later Bryusov admitted that the last seven years before the revolution were characterized in the life of Russian poetry almost exclusively by the achievements of the Acmeists.[44]

With recognition as a group came also the desire to obtain a wider medium of expression than the few pages of *Hyperboreos*, which had a limited circulation, could afford. It was the then well-established *Apollon* which in its first issue for 1913 not only published Gumilyov's "manifesto" entitled "The Heritage of Symbolism and Acmeism" and an exposition of the new school by Gorodetsky, but opened its pages hospitably to the entire group. "From then on *Apollon* became the official organ of the new school."[45]

In his "manifesto" Gumilyov wrote:

To take the place of Symbolism comes a new movement, no matter what its name, whether Acmeism (from the word *acme* meaning the highest degree of anything, flower or flowering era) or Adamism (a manly, firm and clear outlook on life), but in any case demanding a greater balance of forces and a more exact knowledge of relationship between the subject and the object than was the case with Symbolism. . . Although valuing the Symbolists highly, because they have taught us the meaning of the symbol in art, we do not consent to sacrifice to it other means of poetical expression and we seek their complete correlation. By this we answer the question about the comparative "beautiful difficulty" of the two movements: it is more difficult to be an Acmeist than a Symbolist as it is more difficult to build a cathedral than a tower. And one of the principles of the new movement is always to follow the line of greatest resistance. . . Each movement experiences an attraction to one or another of the creators or epochs of the past. Graves of dear ones bind people together more strongly than anything else. In circles close to Acmeism the names of Shakespeare, Rabelais, Villon, and Théophile Gautier are mentioned more often than others. Each one of them is a cornerstone of the Acmeist building, a high intensity of one or the other of its elements. Shakespeare showed us the inner life of man, Rabelais the body and its joys, a wise physiological state. Villon told us about life, which has no doubts in the least about itself, yet knows all—God, vice, death, and immortality; for this life Théophile Gautier found in art worthy garments of faultless form. To unite these four moments in one is the dream which binds together those who so boldly have called themselves Acmeists.[46]

To this may be added some excerpts from the article of Sergei Gorodetsky, the most aggressive of the group:

The struggle between Acmeism and Symbolism (if it is really a struggle and not merely the occupation of an abandoned fortress) is primarily a struggle for *this* world—singing, colorful, having form, weight, and time—for our planet the Earth. . . The first step in the manifestation of love for this world was the exotic. As if created anew, animals flooded poetry; the early poems of N. Gumilyov were filled with elephants, giraffes, lions, parrots from the Antilles [cf. D. H. Lawrence]. . . The most difficult task was to lay out a new road to lyricism; the road to epos was not so encumbered, but to a lyricism of faultless words one had to fight one's way. Is it not because of this that Gumilyov's youthful book was entitled "The Way of Conquistadors"? . . . Indeed, one had to have a lot of daring and of unmitigated love for the future in order to profess in lyricism the cold detachment of Théophile Gautier at a time when lyrico-magic poetry had reached its apogee. . . As a new fearless architect, N. Gumilyov decided to use in poetry only "impassionate material". . . . Then, the critics will say, this new poetry is that of the Parnassians? No. These new poets are not Parnassians because they do not value abstract eternity for itself. They are not impressionists either, because every momentary occurrence does not constitute for them an artistic aim in itself. They are also not Symbolists, because they do not seek in every moment a glimpse into eternity. They are *Acmeists*, because they take into art those moments which can become eternal.[47]

These pronouncements were immediately attacked by some of the influential poets of the time. On April 20, 1913, Blok wrote in his diary: " 'There seems to be a new conception of the world in acmeism,' Gorodetsky babbles on the telephone. I say, 'Why do you want to call yourselves something different when there is nothing that distinguishes you from us?' "[48] And Bryusov went one step further. In a lengthy article in the April 1913 issue of *Russkaya Mysl'* he vehemently denounced the newly born Acmeists, concluding that they were a menace to young talents. "However," he added, "this menace cannot be lasting. Most probably in a year or two there will be no trace left of Acmeism."[49] Bryusov proved to be a poor prophet, because the movement not only survived in Russia until the revolution of 1917 (it continued abroad when some of the Acmeists, including Georgi Ivanov, became emigrés), but it also parented the school of neoclassicists in Soviet poetry.[50]

Notwithstanding such criticism with which the pronouncements of the Acmeists were greeted, the new movement soon found itself dominating the Russian literary scene as representing "a new poetical *Weltanschaaung*".[51] This was due not in small measure to Gumilyov's unbounded energy and feverish activity. He not only read his poems at different literary gatherings, but expounded his ideas in literary debates on a number of occasions. On December 19, 1912, he participated in a debate, which followed a lecture on Symbolism and Acmeism by Gorodetsky. He stressed the difference between the two schools—the former represented, in his opinion, the "triumph of the feminine element in spiritual culture, whereas the latter gave a decisive preference to the masculine element."[52]

In the spring and summer of 1913, Gumilyov made his third trip to Africa, visiting this time Abyssinia and Somaliland as the head of an expedition organized by the Academy of Sciences. After returning to Russia in the autumn with a collection of items depicting the life of East African tribes for the Museum of Anthropology and Ethnography, he resumed his literary activity.

On November 30, 1913, he was elected member of the council of the Society of Adepts of the Artistic Word and at the meeting of this society on December 8, 1913, he read his new one-act drama in verse, *Acteon*, which has remained unpublished. Again on January 20, 1914, at the meeting of the same society, while participating in a discussion of a new translation of Aeschylus' *Agamemnon* by Vyacheslav Ivanov, Gumilyov expressed his ideas on the art of the translator and remarked that the first prerequisite of a good translation should be that the "translator be congenial with the original."[53]

It was not presumptuous on the part of Gumilyov to discuss translations, because he was a first-class translator himself. In 1911 he published a critico-biographical article on Théophile Gautier accompanied by translations of four of the latter's poems from *Emaux et Camées*. This was followed by the publication in 1913 of his translation of stanzas XXXVI to XLI from the *Grand testament* of François Villon as well as the latter's "Ballad about Ladies of Bygone Days."[54] Finally, early in 1914, Gumilyov published in book form his complete translation of Gautier's *Emaux et Camées*.

A talented critic, writing about Gumilyov as he was in the years immediately preceding the outbreak of the World War of 1914, remarked: "It seems to me to this day that the greatest monument to Gumilyov of that era is his priceless translation of *Emaux et Camées*, which was indeed a miracle of reincarnation in the image of his beloved Gautier. Taking into consideration the radical difference between the French and Russian art of versification, between the natural rhythm and articulation of both languages, it is impossible to imagine a more striking impression of the identity of the two texts. And do not think that it is possible to reach such complete analogy merely by thoughtfulness and by the perfection of the technique, by a highly developed craft; a greater achievement is needed— an actual poetical brotherhood with a poet of a foreign tongue."[55]

At the February 1914 meeting of the Society of Adepts of the Artistic Word, Gumilyov read his new epic poem *Mik i Lui* consisting of 960 lines (it was published under the title *Mik*). It is the story of an Abyssinian slave-boy, Mik, who is the captured son of a once powerful rival chieftain slain in battle; of Louis, the ten-year-old son of the French consul in Addis-Ababa; and of a large ape, whom Mik has befriended. The trio run away from the Abyssinian capital and in the course of their adventures Louis is proclaimed king of the apes. But, tired of ruling apes, Louis wanders away on his own and is killed by panthers. Mik then is helped by the Spirit of the Forest and eventually returns to Addis-Ababa, not as a slave but as a rich prince, and becomes the trusted adviser of King

Menelik. Such, in brief, is the story of this delightful poetic work in which Louis, representing the white man's supremacy, is at first the uncontested leader but later succumbs to the wild beasts he has aroused, while Mik, the native, triumphs because he has allied himself (not without the supernatural help of the Spirit of the Forest) with the very forces which have destroyed Louis. In the discussion which followed the first reading of this poem, Gumilyov maintained "that the only field in which there are still possibilities for great epics is exotic poetry."[56]

When the war broke out in August 1914, Gumilyov immediately entered the armed forces, although he was not subject to the draft. He joined the guards regiment of Her Majesty's Uhlans and was assigned to Her Majesty's squadron.[57] This pleased Gumilyov very much, because he had always been a staunch monarchist[58] and even when talking about art had often drawn on his monarchist vocabulary, as when he said: "Literature is lawful and beautiful like a constitutional state, but inspiration is the autocrat who is enchanting because his living soul is above iron laws."[59]

At first a private and later a non-commissioned officer, Gumilyov was commissioned a second lieutenant of the Empress Alexandra Fifth Hussar Regiment on April 10, 1916, after twice winning the Cross of St. George, the most coveted military decoration of Imperial Russia, which was bestowed for personal bravery beyond the line of duty, [60] like the Victoria Cross of Great Britain or the Congressional Medal. Proudly he exclaimed in one of his later poems:

> Twice Saint George has touched the breast
> Which was untouched by any bullet.

The war was a great experience for Gumilyov. His talent literally was tempered in the fire of battle. "He was the first one among Russian poets to write a poem glorifying war. It is a pity even to see these wonderful verses in print. They should be sung to 'victory's resounding trumpet.' "[61]

The Sun of Spirit

How could we live before in quiet,
Nor wait for joy or for misfortune,
Nor dream about the fiery battle
Or victory's resounding trumpet?

How could we? But 'tis not too late:
The sun of spirit shines above us,
The sun of spirit, kind and dread,
The vastness of the skies has covered.

The spirit flowers like a rose,
Like fire it tears through former darkness;
The body blindly following,
Without regret or understanding.

In wild delights of open steppes,
In quiet mysteries of forests—
There's nothing that the will finds hard,
Or that the soul could call a torture.

I feel that fall will soon be here
And bring the end to sunny labors;
Then men will pick the golden fruit
That ripened on the tree of spirit.

Similar feelings are expressed in another war poem:

The Attack

What might have been a paradise
Has now become a den of fire.
Four days on end we've been attacking,
All foodless in the snow and mire.

There is no need of earthly food
In this strange hour of light and dread,
Because the mighty living word
Is better food to us than bread.

And all the blood-empurpled weeks
Are dazzling and their burden light.
The shrapnels rush above my head
With fragments swift as birds in flight.

When I call out, my voice is wild.
Brass striking brass is in my cry.
Upholder of a lofty thought,
I cannot, no, I cannot die.

As 'twere the sound of thundering hammers
Or waters of the raging sea,
The golden heart of valiant Russia
Beats in my bosom evenly.

And oh, it is so sweet to deck
Victory, like a maid, with pearls,
When moving down the smoking track
As the defeated foe recoils.[62]

During the first years of the war (1915-1916) Gumilyov
also wrote regular articles from the front under the general
title "Zapiski kavalerista" (Notes of a Cavalryman) in a Petrograd daily newspaper, *Birzhevye Vedomosti* (The Stock-Ex-
change Journal). [63] But not all of Gumilyov's inspiration during that time came from war themes. During a furlough in
Petrograd he attended a meeting of the Society of Adepts of
the Artistic Word on December 12, 1915, and read some of
his new lyrics. In this period Gumilyov was also at work on
a poem in dramatic form entitled *Ditya Allakha* (Child of
Allah) and containing 756 lines, which he read for the first

time at a special convocation in the editorial offices of *Apollon* on March 19, 1916.[64] In this imaginative Arabian fairy tale a divine peri descends to earth with Allah's permission to become the bride of the best of the humans. A handsome youth, a beduin, a sheik, a cadi, a caliph and his son, a pirate, and Sindbad seek to win her charms in turn but they all perish because each one of them has some defect. At length, the divine peri is won by Hafiz-the-Poet, who in his utter goodness makes her restore life to her former unfortunate suitors, but they all refuse to come back to earth having found a much more interesting place in the afterworld. Then Hafiz-the-Poet, whose calling is the highest among Allah's virtues and who loves the earth, and his divinely sent bride, who becomes mortal of her own choice, are united in love. Such a simple story gives Gumilyov the opportunity to write beautiful verse, skillfully introducing some genuine oriental meters.

Gumilyov's fifth book of verse, *Kolchan* (The Quiver), appeared in 1916. Although Gumilyov wrote

> From "The Romantic Flowers" to "The Quiver"
> I'm still the same old self

Kolchan shows Gumilyov's maturity as a poet. "In it he has grown into a great and discriminating artist of the word."[65] The forty-four poems collected in this book are of different value and of different inspiration. Chronologically speaking, they cover the four years of Gumilyov's development since the publication of *Chuzhoe Nebo*. Some of them had previously appeared in *Apollon* and *Russkaya Mysl'*, and one actually bears the date 1912-1915. Eleven of the poems deal with Italy (including an ode to d'Annunzio), five with the war, one with China, and only two with Africa. Among the others there are three that are outstanding. In one of them, written before the war of 1914, the poet speaks of his loneliness (and Gumilyov was a lonely soul, though always surrounded by people, as testified by his friend and pupil Georgi Ivanov[66]):

> With present life I am quite civil,
> But there's a barrier between us:
> My real delight is in what makes
> The haughty one ridiculous.
>
> Victory, glory, sacrifice—
> Pale words forgotten here at present—
> Sound in my soul like thunderbolts,
> Like God's own voice in the lost desert.
>
> . . .
>
> But no, I am no tragic hero—
> I am ironical, more matter of fact.
> Yet I am mad as a bronze idol
> Who sits among some china dolls.

In another poem—"One of the most remarkable poems ever written" in the opinion of Vladimir Nabokov, the talented contemporary poet—Gumilyov's muse is more buoyant, more hopeful, although this poem too ends on a note of resignation:

> *Stanzas*
>
> This island has such dizzy heights,
>   Such misty shores!
> And the Apocalypse was written here
>   And here Pan died.
>
> But there are those with groves of palms,
>   Where work is gay,
> And where there roams with tinkling bells
>   A flock of sheep.

A violin of forms divine—
    Holding my breath,
I took and listened how her soul
    Flowed into sound.

'Tis only magic that by fate
    I'm daily slain,
That nightly stars rain o'er my head
    'Midst din and groans.

I'm free, trusting my fate again—
    The world's my home.
I kiss a girl with a warm face
    And avid mouth.

An instant only joining us,
    The bridge is down.
The crosses, swords, and cups of stars
    Will burn it up.

In the third poem the call of the sea is beautifully if nostalgically expressed:

Today I heard again the sound
Of anchors rattling heavily,
And then I saw a noble ship
Put out for lands across the sea.
For this the sun breathed brighter light
And earth was like a song to me.

And can there be a single rat
In dirty galley or worm in hole,
Or any mortal, toothless, bald,
Pursuing money as his goal,
Who does not hear Ulysses' song
Calling to play where oceans roll?

To play with merry Neptune's trident,
With flowing locks of naiads wild,
When breakers stir like ringing chords
And break sonorously or glide
With trembling foam about the breast
Of Aphrodites young and mild?

I too will leave my anchored house
And go toward another fate.
A world, both alien and familiar,
Is there to greet me at the gate:
The winding shores, the wild ravines,
Wind and the sea immaculate.

The sun of the spirit never sets,
'Tis not for earth its power to quell.
And nevermore will I return:
The flesh will lose its ancient spell,
If summer to my quest is kind
And I am loved by Heaven as well.[67]

But it is in his poems about the war (including the two mentioned above) that Gumilyov has shown his greatest growth. War as a serious, stern, and holy affair, in which the whole force of an individual soul and the total value of a determined human will are revealed before the face of death—such is the mood of these poems. They are impregnated by a profound religious spirit.

Kolchan was received enthusiastically by the critics, some of whom devoted to it entire articles or the major parts of articles.[68] Only one voice was raised in sharp criticism, accusing Gumilyov of rhetoric, of verbosity, of misuse of words, of lack of sense of measure, of having abandoned his "muse of distant travels" and thrown himself headlong into a religious pessimism. "To such critics," wrote Zhirmunsky, "Gumilyov has the right to answer:

> Victory, glory, sacrifice—
> Pale words forgotten here at present—
> Sound in my soul like thunderbolts,
> Like God's own voice in the lost desert."[69]

In 1916 Gumilyov wrote a great dramatic poem in four acts, *Gondla*. The action of the poem takes place in far-off Iceland in the ninth century. By way of introduction Gumilyov presented quotations from the works of two authors: one a Russian, the other a Frenchman. Since these quotations actually constitute "program notes" to the poem they are given here in full:

In Iceland, on that distant northern island, which belongs to the New rather than to the Old World, two original cultures—the Norman and the Celtic (both alien to us)—came to a clash in the ninth century. There, almost under the Arctic Circle, Scandinavian Vikings and Irish hermits met; the former were armed by swords and battle axes, the latter by monk's staffs and the Holy Book. This accidental encounter seems to have predestined the future history of the island, a history of a spiritual fight between the sword and the Gospel, which transformed the mighty sea kings of the ninth century into the peaceful gatherers of birds' feathers, fishermen and shepherds of our days.   —S. N. Syromyatnikov.

The primitive German revolts us by his unwarranted rudeness, by his love for evil, which makes him clever and strong only for hatred and destruction. The Celtic knight, on the other hand, was always directed even in his strange deviations by habits of goodwill and compassion to the weak. This feeling is one of the deepest in the Celtic people; they had pity even for Judas . . .   —Ernest Renan[70]

The plot of the story is simple. Gondla, a hunchback, who is supposed to be the son of an Irish king, is married for state reasons to the daughter of an Icelandic chief, but one of the young Icelandic warriors consummates the marriage before Gondla reaches the bridal chamber. Instead of challenging his rival, Gondla appeals to the chief for justice and asks that the perpetrator of the outrage be punished. But the chief repulses him because Gondla has refused to fight and thus has violated the code of honor of Iceland. He is ostracized and then the story is revealed that he is not the son of a king but a nobody who was substituted for the real prince when the latter was washed overboard during the passage from Ireland. After this becomes known, he is persecuted and has to flee and hide in the forest. Then a detachment of Irish warriors arrives to seek Gondla, whose father, an Irish bard, had been elected king. But rather than return to his native land, Gondla, who has really fallen in love with his bride, attempts by the power of his word to convert the Icelanders to Christianity. When he fails, he immolates himself on the altar of his cause by driving a sword into his own breast. Following his death, the Icelanders are converted when they kiss, one by one, the hilt of the sword which protrudes in the shape of a cross from Gondla's breast, while Lera, Gondla's bride, who has finally become aware of the greatness of Gondla's soul, prepares to follow him into death by sailing with his body into the endless ocean.

Written in immaculately beautiful verse, the poem is a natural development of Gumilyov's religious attitude, which had already appeared so strongly in his war poems. Precisely for this reason it was severely criticized by a leading critic of Soviet Russia.[71] Nevertheless, it is one of the outstanding examples of the best in modern Russian literature. Early in 1922, six months after Gumilyov was executed, an experimental theater in Petersburg produced *Gondla*. But when the public clamored "Author! Author!" the Soviet authorities ordered the performance closed.

After the March 1917 revolution, Gumilyov was sent on May 30 to the Saloniki front, but he never reached his destination as he was ordered to remain in Paris, where he had arrived on July 14. There he served as adjutant to the Provisional Government's special commissar attached to the Russian troops on the Western Front. In the early spring of 1918, after the Bolsheviks had been in power for almost six months, Gumilyov returned to Russia.[72] He was no longer in the army and he resumed as a civilian his activity as a poet.

"I recall the alleys of the Summer Garden at Petrograd, the spring breezes from the Neva, the tramway bells from the Champs de Mars, the statues grizzled by time, and the quiet sarcasm of Gumilyov's discourse. This was in April 1918—our last interview. . . Gumilyov spoke of the Bolsheviks ironically, without hatred."[73] And he devoted his energies to teaching young poets how to write good verse. He was severely criticized at times then and since for his insistence (both with himself and with his pupils) that poetry should follow strongly defined canons. "But why it should be harmful to the poet to do what is absolutely essential to the musician or the painter, not one of his attackers has ever clarified. However, some of our critics who are still clinging to our old-fashioned Asiatic ways in which 'perhaps,' 'maybe,' and 'somehow' are revered as a commandment, have expressed in all possible ways their displeasure at the work of this laborious and cultured European in the dense thickets of the Russian artistic word."[74]

During 1918 he published a new book of verse, *Kostyor* (The Bonfire), his Abyssinian poem *Mik*, his Arab tale *Ditya Allakha*, and a collection of Chinese poems adapted from

French and English translations under the title of *Farforovy Pavil'on* (The Porcelain Pavilion).

Of the twenty-nine poems in *Kostyor* only three had been previously published in *Apollon*.[75] Among the others, four were inspired by Scandinavia, through which Gumilyov had traveled on his trip to France in 1917, and only one by Africa. The tone of *Kostyor* is subdued. As one Soviet critic remarked: "The October [November] revolution which destroyed the class to which Gumilyov was bound, strengthened his feeling of doom. The theme of despair and of death, which had been sounded before in Gumilyov's poetry, received now an even sharper treatment. This conditioned also Gumilyov's artistic evolution. After the October [November] revolution he veers sharply to the style of the Symbolists and to a mystical content."[76] There is a nostalgic note in such poems as "Stockholm," at the end of which the poet exclaims:

> And then I understood that I had lost my way
> Forever in blind passages of space and time,
> And that somewhere my native rivers flow,
> The road to which is always barred for me.

And in another, entitled "Trees,"[77] Gumilyov sounds a note almost of despair when he says:

> I know it is to trees and not to us
> The greatness of a perfect life belongs.
> On this kind earth, a sister to the stars,
> We live in foreign lands and they at home.
>
> . . .
>
> Oh, if I could only find a land
> In which I need not weep, nor sing, nor suffer,
> While rising silently to lofty heights
> Through all this world's incalculable ages.

41

But there are poems of a brighter mood also, full of genuine religious reverence, and yet very much of this earth. The following is an example:

Second Canzone

Thy temple, Lord, is in the heavens,
But earth is also Thy abode.
The linden trees bloom in the forests,
And birds upon them sing Thy glory.

Like the ringing of church bells, spring
Comes over gay and emerald fields;
And in the spring on wings of dreams
The angels fly to comfort us.

If that is so, oh! Lord, I pray,
If I sing rightly Thine own song,
I pray, oh! Lord, give me a sign,
That I have understood Thy will.

Then before her, who now is sad,
Appear, oh! Lord, like Light Unseen,
And to all questions she will ask
Give her a dazzling reply.

Because more pleasant than birds' songs,
More glorious than the angel's trumpet,
To us are smiles of loved lips,
And fleeting tremblings of eyelashes.

On the whole *Kostyor* reflects Gumilyov's changing and changeable mood of that time, although technically his poetry has taken a step forward as compared with *Kolchan*.

In 1919, that "hungry," desolate year of war communism, Gumilyov published an immaculate translation of a Babylonian epic poem, "Gilgamesh," which he had completed as early as 1918. It is not a "scientific" translation, as Gumilyov said himself, since he had used for his original the work of Paul Dhorme, *Choix de textes religieux assyrobabyloniens: Transcription, traduction, commentaire* (Paris, 1907), but it is a beautiful poetical work. The same year saw the publication of Gumilyov's translation of *The Rime of the Ancient Mariner* by Coleridge.

During the next two years Gumilyov devoted most of his energies to the publishing enterprise World Literature, organized by Maxim Gorky for the purpose of publishing in popular form translations of all the masterpieces of world literature. He was a member of the governing board of this enterprise.[78] But he was not forgetting his calling as a teacher of the younger generation of poets. In addition to a group of poets calling themselves the Sounding Sea-Shell, which united Acmeists, Symbolists, and romanticists, and of which Gumilyov was "an honorary syndic,"[79] he directed half a dozen proletarian poetry clubs, formed by workers of factories and mills, to whom he imparted his profound knowledge of poetical technique. Notwithstanding the fact that through this activity Gumilyov had to deal with Soviet authorities, he did not compromise his political beliefs. He even dared to recite to his proletarian students verses in which he tells of a visit to the Negro chief of the tribe of Galla in Somaliland to whom he presented "a Belgian pistol and the portrait of my Sovereign Emperor."

Throughout these years Gumilyov maintained himself aloof from the events of the times. The poet Vladislav Khodasevich tells an interesting story about him: "During Christmas in 1920 the Institute of the History of Art organized a ball. I remember the enormous icy cold rooms of the Zubov palace in the square of St. Isaacs, scantily lighted and filled with frosty vapors. Green logs fizzled and smoked in the fireplaces. The whole of literary and artistic Petersburg was present. The music thundered. People moved about in semi-darkness, pressed close to the fireplaces. My God, how they were dressed! Felt boots, sweaters, well-worn fur coats which could not be discarded even in the ball room. And then, sufficiently late, appeared Gumilyov with his wife in a deep décolleté dress on his arm. Straight and haughty, in white tie and tails, Gumilyov made the rounds. He may have been shivering under his stiff shirt, but he bowed right and left with a majestic amiability. He talked to his acquaintances in a high society manner. His whole demeanor seemed to say: 'Nothing has happened. A revolution? I for one have not heard about it.' " [80]

Toward the end of 1920 he was drawn into the fatal conspiracy, which cost him his life. But shortly before his arrest, in the summer of 1921, he published almost simultaneously his two most important poetical works: *Ognenny Stolp* (The Pillar of Fire), dedicated to his second wife, Anna Nikolayevna Engelhardt, and *Shatyor* (The Tent), a collection of sixteen African poems never before published. *Ognenny Stolp* consists of twenty poems—each one a masterpiece. Here we see a perfect example of that "cult of the word as such, its valuation not on its musical properties alone, but as a complicated and indestructible unit, which formed the essence of Acmeism." [81] This is best revealed in a poem entitled "The Word"—one of the best of all Gumilyov's poems—in which the poet laments the misuse of this greatest human, nay divine, instrument:

> In those days, when o'er his new creation
> God was lowering his face, men then
> With a word could stop the sun's own progress,
> With a word destroy reluctant towns.
> . . .

And for common life there were the numbers,
Like domestic, well-behaved cattle.
Since all shades of meaning can be rendered
By a clever number used with skill.

. . .

But we did forget that shining brightly
Among earthly ills there is the word,
That Saint John in opening his Gospel
Said to us: The word is truly God.

We, however, limited its greatness
By the limits of our present self.
And, like bees in an abandoned hive,
Dead words smell of death, decay and rot.

In another poem—"Memory"—Gumilyov treats the problem of reincarnation in reverse:

Only serpents cast their skins off,
So that the soul should mature and grow.
We, alas! are not like serpents,
We keep our bodies and change our souls.

With a giant's hand you, memory,
Lead our life like a bridled steed;
You will tell me who before me
In my body spent his earthly days.

Then the poet recalls the souls which had inhabited his body: a dreamer, a poet, an adventurer—a seafarer and hunter, the favorite of the three. But in his present incarnation the poet cannot discern which of the three has prevailed. And he ends:

I'll cry out . . . but who can help it
So that my soul should live and not die.
Only serpents cast their skins off,
We keep our bodies and change our souls.

45

In the most talked-of poem of the book—"The Trolley Car That Lost Its Way"—a somewhat nightmarish, yet beautiful composition, Gumilyov "reflected the contemporary scene and his feeling of it."[82] One has a sense of unreality in it, almost of a glimpse into the great beyond, and it seems that in it Gumilyov prophetically foresaw his own death:

> Down a strange street I aimlessly wandered,
> When the caw of ravens I heard from afar,
> And the peals of a lute, to which thunder responded—
> There flew before me a trolley car.
>
> How I jumped on it as past it thundered,
> Gaining a foothold, is dim in my mind.
> Tearing the air in the daylight asunder,
> Streaking with fire the path left behind;
>
> Whirling like storm clouds, darker and darker,
> In the chasm of time it lost its way...
> Please stop the trolley car, conductor,
> Please stop the car right away!
>
> But too late. Round a bend we have traveled,
> Through a palm grove we've furrowed a lane,
> And we roared over bridges of marble—
> 'Cross the Neva, the Nile, and the Seine.
>
> Then flashing past the frame of the window
> An old beggar-man—the same, I know,
> Threw after us a look that dwindled.
> He died in Beirut a year ago.
>
> Where am I now? With alarming langor,
> My heart beats in answer: There you see
> A depot where midst the noise and clangor,
> To the Land of Souls you can buy a seat.

Here is a sign-board . . . Blood-filled letters
Proclaim it's a grocer's, but I know—
Instead of cabbages, turnips, and lettuce,
Here they sell dead-heads all in a row.

Red of shirt, with a face like an udder,
The headsman cut off my head, too.
And it lay there, right next to the others,
In a slippery box as in glue.

And in a lane—a fence with a marker,
A house with three windows, pale and grey . . .
Please stop the trolley car, conductor,
Please stop the car right away!

Máshenka, here you did live, my song-bird;
Here you did weave a carpet, my bride.
Where then are now your voice and your body?
How can it be that you also have died?

Oh! how you moaned in your bed-chamber,
When in a powdered wig I went
To be presented to the Great Empress,*
Never to see you or hear your lament.

Now it is clear that freedom's a semblance,
Only a light which streams from beyond.
People and shadows stand at the entrance
Into a Zoo of planets in bond.

Then comes a wind, so sweet and beloved,
And beyond the bridge there flies at me
The hand of the Horseman iron-gloved
And the raised hoofs of his steed.†

---

*The poet alludes to Catherine II the Great, Empress of Russia, notorious in later life for picking young men as lovers.

†This is a reference to the famous equestrian statue of Peter the Great erected in St. Petersburg by Catherine the Great.

Guarding the true faith stands like a castle
St. Isaac's Cathedral* for all to see;
There I'll attend a "Te Deum" for Másha,
And a "Requiem" mass for me.

And still the heart is sullen forever,
Hard it's to breathe, painful to live . . .
Máshenka, I did not think that ever
One could so love and so grieve.

Ognenny Stolp contains also a poem in free verse (a rare
form for our poet) entitled "My Readers," "in which can be
felt the old Gumilyov"[83] and in which he gives a sort of analysis
of his poetical work.

An old adventurer in Addis-Ababa,
Who had conquered many tribes,
Sent to me a black spear-bearer
With a greeting composed of my poems.
A lieutenant, who had commanded gunboats
Under the fire of enemy batteries,
Through a whole night in the South Seas
Recited my poems by heart.
A man, who in a crowd of people
Had shot an emperor's envoy,
Came to me to press my hand
And to thank me for my poems.

Then he explains why they like his poetry, and by doing so
gives a key to our own understanding of his philosophy of
strength and will power:

I teach them how not to fear,
Not to fear and do what one must.

---

*This is a reference to the majestic shrine built in St. Petersburg in
the reign of Nicholas I.

And when a woman with a beautiful face,
The dearest face in the whole universe,
Will say: I do not love you—
I teach them how to smile,
And to go away, never to return.
And when their last hour comes
And a steady red fog dims their eyes,
I shall teach them how to remember at once
This whole life, cruel yet kind,
This whole earth, ours yet strange,
And, having appeared before the face of God,
Who has only simple and wise words,
How calmly to await his last judgment.

There is no doubt in this writer's mind that *Ognenny Stolp* is one of the greatest books of poetry ever written. And a contemporary literary critic writes: "*Kostyor* and *Ognenny Stolp* show us the poet grown to his full stature, having reached creative maturity. But even now, having seen death face to face and tasted of the deepest mysteries of existence, he did not turn away from life, from the world which, like God, lives for ever."[84] Next to *Ognenny Stolp* in greatness stands *Shatyor*, which in itself is a unique phenomenon in Russian letters, devoted as it is entirely to poems about Africa. "These poems—the fruit of his African journeys—have been awaited a long time from the poet-explorer. The mere summary of the titles is like a colorful catalogue of geographical names which are provided with living flesh and blood in almost faultless compositions. Indeed, there rises before us a powerful image—Africa herself. . . In any case this is a chapter which the history of world poetry must take into account."[85] So wrote the Soviet critic and poet Innokenty Oksyonov. And, indeed, there are few poems in the world which express Africa as genuinely and beautifully as do Gumilyov's verses in *Shatyor*.

In the rhythm of the poem entitled "Somaliland" one can almost feel the beating of native drums:

I remember that night and the dreary sand,
And the moon in the sky just above that land.

I remember that I could not turn my eye
From its golden way in the glittering sky.

. . .

And that evening as soon as the shadows grew long,
In my ears crept the sound of Somali's war gong.

Their leopard-like chief with a crown of red hair
Was the bringer of death to the white and the fair.

. . .

I knew well that at dawn the arrows would rain,
And I and my slaves would have fought in vain;

But I looked at the moon and thought through the night,
That there I would have no men to fight.

. . .

When the morning came near and the moon sank low—
No more as a friend, but a scarlet foe—

It was clear to me that it shone as a shield
For all the great heroes who fell in the field.

So I ordered my slaves to withdraw and to run,
And I trusted my soul to my Winchester gun.

But it is in the introductory poem, one of the most beautiful of the lot, that Gumilyov reveals his feelings of awe, reverence, and love toward that great dark continent, the opening stanza of which reads:

Deafened by thunder and roaring,
Enveloped in smoke and fires,

Africa, about thee in whispers
In the heavens the seraphs are speaking.

The poet is ready to tell Africa's "frightful and wonderful story," and as a reward he asks:

And for this let me tread a path,
Where before me no man has been;
Let me name after me a stream,
A black stream uncovered as yet.

And at last, as a final grace
To speed me to the holy camp,
Let me die 'neath that sycamore
Where once Mary rested with Christ.

But fate was cruel to Gumilyov; his wish was not fulfilled. Instead he was executed by a firing squad on August 25, 1921, for participating in a conspiracy led by the former senators Tagantsev and Strakhovsky to overthrow the Soviet government.[86] His indictment, as published at the time, read: "Gumilyov, N. S., thirty-three years of age,[87] philologist and poet, member of the governing board of the publishing enterprise World Literature, no party affiliation, a former officer. Collaborated in the writing of proclamations. Promised to connect with the organization a group of intellectuals at the moment of uprising. Received money from the organization for technical purposes."[88]

From his prison cell, when he knew already that there was no hope of his surviving, he wrote to his wife: "Do not worry about me, I feel fine; I am reading Homer and am writing verse." To his tormentors, who asked him continuously why he conspired against the Soviet Government, he answered laconically: "Because I am a monarchist." And by the testimony of his own executioners, he faced the firing squad smiling and died unwaveringly like a hero.[89]

Such is the tragedy of Russian literature that all of its best poets die young and by a violent death at that: Pushkin at thirty-seven, Lermontov at twenty-six, and Gumilyov at thirty-five. Pushkin and Lermontov died from bullets fired in a duel, but why did Gumilyov die?

"In the direct, in the exact meaning of these words Gumilyov sacrificed his life not for the restoration of monarchy, nor even for the regeneration of Russia—he died for the regeneration of poetry. He firmly believed that the right to call oneself a poet belongs only to the one who will strive in every human endeavor to be ahead of others; who, knowing more than the others of all human weaknesses—egotism, pettiness, fear of death—will show in his own example the daily victories over the 'feeble Adam.' He sacrificed himself for the immovable human will, for the highest conception of human honor, for the overcoming of the fear of death, for everything that, notwithstanding all the talent in Russian and world literatures of the last few decades, is completely lacking in them. Gumilyov died in an attempt to hold by his own feeble hands, by his own personal example, that greatest manifestation of the human spirit—poetry—on the brink of a precipice into which it was ready to crash."[90]

Today Gumilyov's works are unobtainable in the Soviet Union since they have not been republished and are not likely to be. But the spirit of this poet of manly inspiration, of brilliant imagination, and of masterly technique is still alive and, believably, is striving to lead Russian poetry out of its new "Babylonian captivity" toward the shining heights of achievement in perfection—Acmeism.

CHAPTER TWO

AKHMATOVA

Oh, there exist such unrepeatable remarks;
The one who spoke them said too much already.
Since inexhaustible are only the blue skies
And God's own mercy so reliable and steady.
                    —Akhmatova, *Belaya Staya*

ANNA AKHMATOVA

Poetess of Tragic Love

It was a wintry evening in 1911. The weekly Wednesday
gathering at the "Tower," the residence of the erudite poet
Vyacheslav Ivanov, was in full swing. Here the flower of the
St. Petersburg poetical world was represented. Poets well established, those less well established, and the beginners recited
in turn and awaited the verdict of the host. Usually this verdict
was politely deadly. The sentence thus pronounced was miti-
gated only by the realization that it was always to the point
and always just. Hence even the slightest approval was a triumph for the victim.

That evening the turn came for a young woman, tall, thin,
dark, with exquisite hands and a striking face. Her name was
Anna Andreyevna Gorenko and she had only recently married
the poet Nicholas Gumilyov. For a pen-name she had chosen
Anna Akhmatova, the name of her great-grandmother who was
a Tartar. She was one of the beginners and as yet unknown,
though some of her verse, read in small literary circles, had
received condescending approval of the well established and
less well established poets—all save her own husband who
looked upon her poetry as the fancy of a poet's wife, although
it was he who published her first poems in his review *Sirius*.

Akhmatova rose, and read in a hesitating voice:

> My heart grew chill so helplessly,
> Although my footsteps seemed so light.
> In all my anguish I was drawing
> My left-hand glove upon my right.
>
> There seemed to be so many steps,
> Although I knew there were but three.
> The breath of autumn in the maples
> Seemed to whisper: "Die with me!
>
> I have been deceived by fate,
> That has neither faith nor rue."
> And I answered in a whisper:
> "So have I. I'll die with you!"
>
> This is the song of our last meeting.
> I glanced toward the house in the night:
> Only the bedroom lights were burning
> With an uncaring yellow light.[1]

Akhmatova sat down. There was a moment's silence. Then Vyacheslav Ivanov got to his feet, crossed the room to where Akhmatova sat waiting and, kissing her hand, said: "Anna Andreyevna, I congratulate you and welcome you. This poem is an event in Russian literature."[2]

A year later, in the spring of 1912, Akhmatova published her first book of poems entitled *Vecher* (Evening) and it was an immediate success. It was supplied with a preface by the poet Mikhail Kuzmin who had given his formula for good poetry: "Love the word as Flaubert did; be economical in your means and avaricious in the use of words; be precise and genuine; and you will find the secret of a divine thing—beautiful clarity."[3]

Reviewing her book a contemporary critic wrote: "Anna Akhmatova knows how to follow the highway of contemporary artistic culture with such primitive independence of her personal life as if this highway were merely a whimsical path in her own private garden. . . Revery feeds the poetry of Anna Akhmatova, a deeply sad revery often romantic in its content. However, we call a romantic a man who sees in reality merely a pretext for revery, but a woman who wants to abandon herself 'to revery is not a romantic but simply—a woman." And years later, when introducing Akhmatova at a recital in Moscow in April 1924, another critic remarked: "On the eve of the fateful crucial epoch of European history, two years before the beginning of the World War, there occurred in Russian literature an event the meaning of which did not reveal itself to us until much later. At the very beginning of 1912 there appeared a slim book of poetry in a grey cover bearing the unpretentious title *Vecher* and signed by the as yet unknown name of Anna Akhmatova. This was one of the most important dates in the annals of our contemporary poetry."[4]

Vecher reads like an intimate diary of a woman in love, "but this intimacy goes beyond the limits of a personal confession, just as everything which is truly and fundamentally personal is thereby also social; the subjective, in completing the circle, returns to the objective."[5] Akhmatova speaks about simple earthly happiness and about simple intimate and personal sorrow. Love, love's parting, unrequited love, love's betrayal, clear and serene confidence in the lover, feelings of grief, of loneliness, of despair—all the things that everyone might feel and understand, though perhaps less deeply and personally than the poet—such are Akhmatova's themes, told with a remarkable frugality:

I pressed my hands beneath the veil . . .
"Why are you so pale today?"
—Because I gave him bitter grief
Till he was drunk with wild dismay.

How shall I forget? He staggered
Away, his mouth awry with pain.
I rushed out after him and ran
Up to the gate in the little lane.

"It was all a joke! If you go away,
I'll die!" I shouted out of breath.
He smiled a sad, quiet smile and said:
"Don't stand in the wind!" This was like death.[6]

Akhmatova's first book was issued by the Guild of Poets, an Acmeist society. But Akhmatova was an Acmeist not only through her early association with the movement; the preciseness and selection of words in their true, fundamental, and not transitory sense—a basic characteristic of the Acmeists—are early traits of her poetry. Perhaps more so than was the case of other Acmeists, hers is "the language of objects—an extraordinary and intimate language."[7] In the opinion of another contemporary critic her art is "fully defined by the concept of plasticity; all methods of her technique, all effects of her verbal expression are conditioned by it."[8] And this concreteness and plasticity of word-images together with new rhythms, which the critic Zhirmunsky compared with the music of Debussy,[9] so pleased the Russian reading public that her book was sold out in record time and her name was soon on the lips of lovers of poetry throughout the length and breadth of Russia.

There is very little biographical data available about Anna Akhmatova. She was born in 1888 in Odessa, the daughter of an officer of the merchant marine.[10] As a child she was brought to Tsarskoye Selo when her father was appointed to the department of the merchant marine in St. Petersburg. She attended the public schools there and later was a pupil of the exclusive Smolny Institute. She completed her secondary education in Kiev and later attended college, first in Kiev and then in St. Petersburg. The accomplishment of her youth she was most proud of was swimming.[11] But she began to write poetry as a child and later remembered as one of her first poems one written at the age of eleven. She met Gumilyov while still in school and married him in 1910.[12] In the years before and during World War I she lived with her husband in a large, comfortable house in Tsarskoye Selo and participated in the gay bohemian literary life of St. Petersburg. Most of what we know about her life in those years we derive from her poetry in which imaginary themes are often intertwined with real happenings.

Fame did not change Akhmatova's life or make it more happy. She was young, but there was a constant tired look around her eyes and her mouth. It was at this time that the painter Nathan Altman painted a portrait of Akhmatova, whose profile was "the dream of a cubist" according to a remark by a contemporary. She was painted on a background of unpleasantly vivid green leaves and grass. Thin, tall, and pale she sat staring icily with dark-ringed eyes, as if she did not notice her surroundings. Her collar bones protruded sharply. Black bangs, as if lacquered, covered her forehead almost to the eyebrows. Colorless, swarthy cheeks, a pale red mouth, thin transparent nostrils completed the picture. And all features and forms were in angles: an angular mouth, an angular bend of the back, angular fingers, angular elbow. Even the high instep of her long slender foot was at an angle. But the portrait was a striking resemblance and more than any other portrait of Akhmatova painted since, it revealed not only her outer form but her inner being as well. It also added to her fame, although Akhmatova herself did not like this painting. No one who had seen the painting ever failed to recognize her when visiting The Cave of the Wandering Dog, a famous artists' night club in St. Petersburg, and seeing Akhmatova in the wee hours of the morning in a corner by the fireplace sipping black coffee and smoking a long thin cigarette.

It was in the spring of 1914—two years after the publication of her first book—that Akhmatova's second book was published. It was entitled *Chyotki* (The Rosary) and included, in addition to new poems, some selections from *Vecher*. It was even a greater success than her first book. Every year, despite war and revolution, saw a new edition, the fifth appearing in 1918, and the eighth in 1922. There was not a single reader or lover of poetry in Russia who had not read her verse. The younger generation simply idolized her. Her success now was greater than that of any other Russian poet, although her themes remained the same. As a Soviet critic put it: "The masterly chiseled poetry of Akhmatova is very poor in ideological content and in social problems raised therein."[13] But the Russian reader of those years was not interested in ideologies and social problems. What attracted him in Akhmatova's poetry was the spontaneity of feeling and the humane, feminine touch of her lyre. A thoughtful poet-critic, N. V. Nedobrovo, said that in order to understand Akhmatova, one should stress in the phrase "woman-poet" the first word and then would come the revelation of her true charm. Akhmatova's poetry is particularly charming, he continued, because "throughout this man-made civilization of ours, love in poetry has been treated so much from the point of view of a man and so little from the point of view of a woman."[14] And Akhmatova was consistent in her femininity. "No poetess ever existed who did not attempt to place herself in a man's position relative to the world or its demands. But Akhmatova remains always a woman either in the description of her own feelings or in her outlook on the beauties around her and the world's mystery and misery."[15] She looked upon the world, whether the world outside or her own inner world of feelings and emotions, with wide open eyes. "Faithful in this sense to the precepts of Acmeism, she could have repeated after Théophile Gautier: 'I belong to those for whom the visual world does exist' . . . Truly the poetess had the right to say about herself: 'I notice everything as if it were new' "[16]

Chyotki opens with a poem called "Perplexity":

> It was stifling from the burning light,
> And his glances were like rays . . .
> I shuddered. This one might
> Tame me by unknown ways.
>
> He is bending. He's to speak again.
> Blood rushed away from my face.
> Let love on my life remain
> Like a slab in the burying place.

In a few words, in a few lines, Akhmatova tells a whole story. "This epigrammatical quality of her verbal forms is one of the most important peculiarities of Akhmatova's poetry. She can paint a Mona Lisa portrait in two lines:

> I have just one peculiar smile,
> Just a tiny movement of lips.

In this lies her resemblance to the French poets of the eighteenth century and the poetry of French classicism in general. In this also lies her deep difference from the musical and emotional lyricism of the romantics and of the Symbolists."[17]

Commenting on the second poem in *Chyotki* the literary historian and critic, Leonid Grossman, wrote:

In the poetic field of love which has been exploited, it seems, to the full by world poetry, Akhmatova found an unknown note which conceived these immortal formulae of the human spirit. They are eternal, indeed, because from the depth of centuries a kindred voice sometimes reaches us, which interprets this undying theme in the same way. Here Akhmatova often approaches, probably unconsciously and unintentionally, the strains of ancient poetry. Such is her little fragment:

> You don't love, you don't wish to look.
> How beautiful, damned, you are!
> And I cannot leave my nook,
> Though since youth I could wing afar.
>
> A mist will bedim my eyes,
> Faces and things will be blurred . . .
> Only the tulip's red rise
> In your buttonhole speaks the word.

In a similar vein Sappho paints the moment of capture of a woman's soul by love:

> My tongue is numb, love's flame
> Embraces me, darkness clouds my eyes,
> I see no light and I can hear and hear only
> A distant rustling . . . .

Thus across twenty centuries the voices of two poetesses meet.[18]

Akhmatova's poetry, particularly in *Chyotki*, has another peculiarity. It is the unexpected but convincing, illogical but fine psychological transitions from words of emotion to words of description, from the soul to nature, from feeling to fact. She assembles artistically the particulars of a given moment which are often unnoticeable to others; she notices everything anew so that her internal world is not merely framed by the external world, but they combine into one solid and organic wholeness of life. "Her poems are her life."[19] She often compares the present with the past, and the recollections of her childhood create nostalgic moods such as this:

On the customs floats a faded flag,
Over the town glides a yellow mist.
My heart beats slowly under a rag,
My lips forever remain unkissed.

To be a little sea girl again,
To put soft slippers on naked feet,
To laugh when dancing under the rain,
And to sing when running down the street;

To look from the steps at the dome aflame
Of the tawny temple of Kersoness,
Unknowing that, spoiled by luck and fame,
Hearts are slowly beating to death.[20]   1913

One can so well imagine how the recollection of her early years in a town on the shores of the Black Sea provoked this emotional comparison with her present life. But the present is strong and it has its rewards, if only it could last.

After braving the wind and frost,
Before a glowing fire I sit.
I care no more about my heart.
Somebody must have stolen it.

The New Year festival goes on,
The New Year roses moistly rise,
And in my breast I hear no more
The flutterings of the dragon-flies.

It is not hard to guess the thief.
I recognized him by his eyes.
I only dread that soon, too soon,
He will himself return the prize.[21]

Akhmatova is essentially an urban poet, primarily a poet of
St. Petersburg. "The spring's twilight—'the white nights'—with
its melancholy and dreaming on the islands, where the Neva
rolls her waves into the sea and where calm and serenity reign;
the autumn winds around the Winter Palace, when smoke from
the chimneys dances a wild witch-dance in the air and the
steel grey Neva roars with hidden fury, streaming over the
parapet into the streets where disaster awaits the citizens of the
capital of Peter the Great; or the cold winter brings down
masses of snow from the grimy sky, covering the pavements
with a white eider down over which horse-drawn sleighs glide
noiselessly—such are the settings of Akhmatova's poetry."[22]
Yet there is something foreboding in the way she speaks about
the city of Peter: "Sumptuous, granite-clad city of glory and
woe"; "dark city by a terrifying river"; "the city loved by a
bitter love." There are also other cities in Akhamatova's poetry
and they are brighter, sunnier: "Hilly Pavlovsk," "brilliant
Tsarskoye Selo," "golden Bakhchisarai."

All told, cities predominate in Akhmatova's poetry. It seems
that man-made structures attract her more than nature's land-
scapes. There is an abundance of cupolas, domes, turrets, towers,
vaults, and arches in her verse. "From her elegies suddenly
and monumentally appear the high vaults of a Catholic church,

palaces, the fortress of Saints Peter and Paul, the arch on Galernaya Street, the white vaults of the Smolny cathedral, the cathedral of St. Isaacs 'in vestments of sterling silver.' Even nature, with its eternal changes, is reflected through the eyes of an artistic builder:

"Autumn as never before built a high dome."[23]

Yet occasionally one finds the picture of a conventional countryside:

There's never a day but it has its excitement.
The smell of the ripening rye's growing stronger.
If, darling, you like lying down at my feet,
Then lie there and rest you a little while longer.

The orioles cry in the wide-spreading maples,
There's nothing will lure them away to the skies.
I like sitting near you and driving away
The wasps that keep flitting about your green eyes.

But hark! There's a harness bell jingling outside.
How sweet are the memories its music can weave!
I'll sing to you, darling, to lighten your sadness,
A sweet little song of our leave-taking eve.[24]

But the country does not keep Akhmatova very long. She is back in St. Petersburg and her setting now is The Cave of the Wandering Dog, the famous artists' night club, gaudily decorated by the painter Sudeikin.

We are revelers, sinners here,
Who can be gay in secret shrouds?
The birds and flowers on the walls
Long for the freedom of the clouds.

You smoke your favorite black pipe.
How odd the smoke above it twines!
And I have donned a tighter skirt
To give my figure slimmer lines.

Forever the windows are blocked up.
Winter or summer behind them lies?
Just like the eyes of a cautious cat
Are your impenetrable eyes.

Oh, how grieving is now my heart!
Does it the mortal hour foretell?
But she, who now is pleased to dance,
Will certainly end in hell.[25]

All these poems are about Gumilyov, her poet-warrior husband, who did not hesitate to leave her for months at a time when going on expeditions into Africa, and who in one of Akhmatova's poems said that "to be a woman-poet is absurd," but whom she loved with a desperate love and to whom she wrote in 1913:

Keep my letters in order that we
Can be judged by our descendants.
So that clearer and more precise
You'd appear to them, wise and courageous:
In your life story—fame, sacrifice—
One should not leave any blank pages.

But she was also fascinated by Alexander Blok, about whom she penned the following lines in 1912:

So helplessly the eyes implore
For mercy. Why do I look so lame
When smiling folk pronounce before me
His crisp and short sonorous name?[26]

And to him she dedicated the following poem written in blank
verse:

> I came visiting the poet.
> Sharp at noon. It was a Sunday.
> In the spacious room it's quiet
> And it's freezing out the window.
>
> There the sun is raspberry colored
> O'er the tattered dark blue smoke ...
> How the silent host is looking,
> Looking so serene at me.
>
> He has eyes that are so tranquil
> That one can't forget them ever.
> As for me it would be wiser
> Not to look at them at all.
>
> But the talk I will remember,
> On a Sunday's smoky noon,
> Near the sea gates of the Neva
> In a tall and grayish house.

In addition there appears a third theme—that of a boy
hopelessly and helplessly in love with her:

> The boy just stammered: "How it aches!"
> It was so sad to see him languish.
> Till recently he'd been so happy,
> Hearsay was all he knew of anguish.
>
> And now he knows it all no less
> Than those of us who've passed that way.
> The pupils of those dazzling eyes
> Have grown so dull they have no ray.

I know he cannot bear his pain,
The first of love that he has known.
How helplessly and eagerly
He strokes my hands as cold as stone.[27]

"These changes of love tunes as well as the whole style of her love are conditioned by the fact that Anna Akhmatova is morally a monastic, a nun with a cross on her breast. She remembers about hell, she believes in God's retribution. Her love is just like a hair-shirt. Her passion is severe and she is troubled by her love, but, perhaps, she is reassured in that her love is unhappy and hence God will not be offended, God will not be outraged by the sinfulness of His worshipper. At that, Akhmatova is a monastic but one living in the world, in the brilliant whirl of the capital, midst refined pleasures, surrounded by outstanding persons—a rare and original combination."[28] And this "monastic" living in the world finds for her lyrics, which are only "a poetization of intimate everyday life,"[29] such words as "are born only once in one's soul," and "a brittle voice" to say them.[30] Reviewing her new book, her poet-husband and critic, Gumilyov, wrote: "In *Chyotki* by Anna Akhmatova the eidolological part is thought through less than anything else. However, the poetess did not try to 'invent herself,' did not place in the center of her experiences, in order to unify them, some outside fact, did not refer to something known or understandable to her alone—she is herself, and in this lies her difference from the Symbolists; on the other hand, her themes are often not carried out fully within the limits of a given poem, much in them appears unfounded, because only half said. . . The most outstanding factor in Akhmatova's poetry is her style: she almost never explains, she demonstrates. . . There are many definitions of color in Akhmatova's poems and most often these are of yellow and of gray, until now the

68

rarest in poetry[31]. . . In comparison with *Vecher* published two years ago, *Chyotki* represents an important step forward. The verse has become more definite, the content of each line more compact, the choice of words chastely restrained."[32]

Even such limited praise from a man who looked upon her art as the fancy of a poet's wife must have pleased Akhmatova. In that year of 1914 she was at the pinnacle of her fame and glory.

And then came the war. Gumilyov volunteered and Akhmatova remained alone in the big house in Tsarskoye Selo with her pink cockatoo, about whom she wrote: "And now I've become as sad as my friend the pink cockatoo." During the war Akhmatova published very few poems, but among them was an "unspeakably beautiful"[33] lyric poem, "By the Very Sea," written in 1914.[34] This poem, the only long poem Akhmatova ever wrote, contains 280 lines and is written in free verse. It is the story of a young, carefree, romantic girl, who lives by the sea and is a friend of the fishermen and of crabs and tarantulas, who can understand the voices of wind and water, and who declines the love of a boy because she awaits the arrival of a prince, of a king's son. The real and the imaginary worlds are intermixed to such an extent that on one hand one could consider this poem to be a fairy tale, and on the other, a very realistic story about a girl who lived more in dreams than in life. The poem ends tragically when the girl finds her prince drowned. The Soviet critic, G. Lelevich, defined it as "a mystic tale about the awaiting of a mysterious bridegroom."[35]

As the war years progressed, a strong religious feeling appears in Akhmatova's verse. She was always deeply religious with a strong, almost primitive, simple faith. And now that death was rampant in the wake of war, now that despair gripped at one's heart when listening to the unfavorable battle news, there was no other recourse than to turn to God for succour. At the first news of the war, Akhmatova, covering her face with her hands, implored God to kill her before the first battle, and exclaimed that the day of declaration of war has made everyone one hundred years older. And now, when she writes about the death of a loved one, she does not rebel at the cruel fate, but merely states that a new warrior has been added to God's own host. "Thy image, thy righteous sacrifice I shall cherish until my hour of death." And she adds:

> It is sinful to cry, it is sinful to languish
> In one's native, beloved house.
> Think, you can now address your prayers
> To your heavenly spouse.

"Such religious submissiveness is typical of Akhmatova's war poems."[36]

It was not until 1917, after the first revolutionary rumble of that year had rolled over Russia, that Akhmatova published her next book, *Belaya Staya* (The White Flock). Most of her themes remained the same as before, but her artistry had become more perfect. Soviet critics have this to say about *Belaya Staya:* "Akhmatova clothes the emotional fullness of her poems in the form of a conversation or a story told to someone present. In striving to make her poetry concrete, sharp, and intimate, Akhmatova not only limits her themes and clothes them in the form of a chat, but also limits the size of her poems. The latter are distinguished by the extreme brevity not only of individual phrases but of the poem as a whole. . . Often the verb is completely absent in Akhmatova's poems as in the following two lines:

> Twenty first. Night. Monday.
> Outlines of the town in mist."[37]

Apparently she took Gumilyov's criticism seriously, for now her themes are more fully carried out within the limits of a given poem, as in the following:

> Before the spring there are such days as these:
> The field reposes underneath the snow,
> A merry noise wakes in the leafless trees,
> And warmer, more elated breezes blow.
>
> You marvel at your body's sudden lightness,
> And hardly recognize your house again;
> And that old song you gave up for its triteness,
> You sing once more just like a new refrain.[38]

And then once more Akhmatova becomes retrospective and compares the days of the present with what is past. Her marriage to Gumilyov was undergoing a crisis and was soon to break up in divorce.

> Instead of wisdom—experience. A tasteless
>   Unsatisfying drink.
> And my youth was like a Sunday prayer—
>   I cannot cease to think.
>
> So many lonely roads traversed
>   With the wrong man.
> So many prayers in churches whispered
>   For him who loved me then.
>
> But I've become completely forgetful.
>   Quietly flow the years.
> Unkissed lips and eyes unsmiling
>   Are beyond reach and tears.

As time goes by, the events of Russia's agony in the war bring forth this outcry of a martyred soul to its Creator:

Prayer

Give me lingering illness for years,
Suffocation, sleeplessness, fever;
Take away both my child and my friend
And the gift of song-writing forever.

Thus I pray at Thy mass every day
After waiting in anguish and worry,
So that storm clouds o'er Russia will soon
Be transformed into laurels of glory.[39]

Later, Russia's surrender to the forces of revolution finds
this echo in Akhmatova's troubled heart:

It seems as if the voice of man
Will never sound here anymore,
And only winds from the stone age
Will knock and knock at the black door.

It seems to me that I alone
Survived under this sky of lead,
Because I was the first to want
To drink the cup of deathly dread.[40]

On the whole, *Belaya Staya*, reflecting the years of war and
revolution, reveal Akhmatova's "brittle voice" as somewhat
subdued, having lost some of the sharpness of *Chyotki*, but mellowed by a religious fatalism so characteristic of a Russian
woman.

Four years had passed since the publication of *Belaya Staya*.
The turmoil of revolution and civil war was gone, but not
forgotten. And then Akhmatova published another book,

Podorozhnik (Buckthorn), very small in size, measuring three by four inches. This pathetic little volume marks a turning point in Akhmatova's poetry. Although the theme of love still predominates, it has now a tragic note. It marks the end of the love of two poets, the end of Akhmatova's marriage to Gumilyov, which had culminated in divorce in 1918, after which Gumilyov remarried. Although Akhmatova herself remarried in later years, her first love remained the stronger.

> I saw the friend to the entrance hall,
> I stood for a while in the golden dust.
> From the belfry nearby a gentle roll
> Of solemn sounds seemed to last and last.
>
> Discarded! That's an invented word—
> Am I a letter or bloom to discard?
> But the mirror's reflection is dim and blurred,
> And the eyes look already stern and hard.

In this little gem more than in Akhmatova's previous poems we find that "the psychic condition, the experience is not revealed directly, but only its symptoms are given in the pose, in the gesture, in the psycho-physiological process which follows it, in the traces of actual objects."[41] Furthermore, the brevity of the whole poem and of each line is remarkable when one considers the fullness of its emotional content and the detailed picturization of its setting. One is really amazed at its mastery.

Similar gems crowd the little pages of *Podorozhnik*, but the significance of the book lies in the fact that for the first time Akhmatova has referred directly to political themes when she wrote in 1919,[42] that year of war communism which Pilnyak called "The Naked Year" in the title of his famous novel:

Why is this age worse than the previous one?
Perhaps because 'midst sadness and alarms
It touched the blackest of all earthly sores,
But could not heal it by its charms?

Still in the West the sun is shining bright
Over the roofs of towns as in the sky;
But here death marks with crosses every house
And calls the ravens, and the ravens fly . . .

Soon after the appearance of *Podoroshnik*, Akhmatova gave a recital of her poems in the House of Men of Letters in red Petrograd. But the small hall could not accommodate even a tenth of those who wanted to hear her. The recital was therefore repeated in the large hall of the University and even then many were left out. The public—a strange mixture of people, some in evening dress, others in sheepskin coats and kerchiefs—crowded the enormous unheated auditorium and listened attentively. "Was it a triumph? No. The majority of listeners were disappointed. They expected to hear that for which they had loved Akhmatova—new left-hand gloves put on the right hand. But they heard something different."[43]

All is plundered, sold, and betrayed,
And the wing of black death is wide-spread;
All is gnawed by a hungry anguish,—
Why then suddenly light shone ahead?

Now in daytime a forest primeval
Softly blows to the town cherry scent,
And at night constellations unheard of
Blaze in depths of a new firmament.

And this wonder comes closer and closer
To the houses in ruin and grime,
Something still so unknown and mysterious,
But desired by us for all time.

"The public was puzzled. They thought: 'It's rank bolshe-vism!' But they applauded politely for old memory's sake, yet thought to themselves: 'She is finished. She has outwritten her-self!' And the critics picked up this 'voice of the people' with sadistic pleasure."[44] But Akhmatova was not finished. The fol-lowing year, 1922, saw the publication of her new book *Anno Domini MCMXXI*, which opened with the poem she had read to her unappreciative audience the year before. Reviewing this book, the Soviet critic Mikhail Pavlov wrote: "The purest, the most moving of all the voices of contemporary poetry and, per-haps, the most human is the voice of Anna Akhmatova."[45]

In a way this book is Akhmatova's swan song, as it is the record of how a woman's love can turn to hate. Its pathos is really tragic and the poetess chose as its epigraph these utterly despairing words: *Nec sine te, nec tecum vivere possum* (Neither without you nor with you can I live). Hapless, tragic love, "love full of evil," marks most of the poems in this book. It is the outcry of a woman abandoned by her lover for another. She curses him for it, and adds threateningly:

And you thought that I am like others,
That one can forget me so soon.

Her love in its unbearable pain has turned to poison and she warns him not to reveal to his new companion the delirium which had possessed them once,

Because it will suffuse with burning poison
Your bountiful, your joyful union.

75

But her hate is only another form of her love, yet there is nothing now she can hope for and so she sighs: "Oh, life without tomorrow!" There is nothing left but despair. "The accursed circle of her personal love and pain is pushed into another, a more frightful circle of all-Russian sorrow which reminds one of the circles of Dante's Inferno."[46] Only in the last poem of this book does there appear a note of religious submissiveness, reminiscent of Akhmatova's war poems, which seems to indicate an exit out of the "accursed circle." In this poem she writes: "I am submissive to God's will alone!" Yet she still rebels against her earthly fate since her submissiveness is "to God's will alone."

Anno Domini seemed to mark the end of Akhmatova's literary career. She stopped publishing, although she did not stop writing. And she remained in Russia. Georgi Ivanov describes movingly his last encounter with her.

1922, autumn. The day after tomorrow I am leaving for Paris. I go to call on Akhmatova to say good-bye. The Summer Garden rustles already autumnally. The Mikhailovsky Castle is bathed in the red glow of the sunset. How empty! How alarming! Good-bye St. Petersburg...

Akhmatova extends her hand to me. Her thin profile is etched on the darkening window. On her shoulders is her famous dark shawl with the pattern of large red roses.

—So you are going away! Give my regards to Paris.

—And you, Anna Andreyevna, aren't you going away?

—No. I shall not leave Russia.

—But it is becoming more difficult to live here with every day.

—Yes, more difficult.

—It may become quite unbearable.

—What if it does!

—So you will not leave?

—No. I shall not leave.[47]

Years went by, but Akhmatova's "brittle voice" remained silent. And then in 1940 there appeared a collection of her selected lyrics under the title *Iz Shesti Knig* (From Six Books), which included an entire new section entitled *Iva* (The Willow). People in the Soviet Union could again read her poems, since her earlier books had been out of print long before. It was still the same Akhmatova, only one endowed with greater wisdom and mellowed by the years, by years of want and of suffering. Her voice was now reduced almost to a whisper and her eyes were dimmed as she looked at the present through the mirror of the past. But her mastery was still the same, as in this short poem written in blank verse:

> When a person is taken by death,
> His portraits undergo a change.
> The eyes look different and the lips
> Smile with a different smile.
>
> I noticed this when returning
> From the funeral of a poet.
> And since then I have tested it often,
> And my guess was each time confirmed.

In a review of this book, the Soviet critic V. Pertsov wrote: "Akhmatova of the year 1940 still writes well. And even better than before. There is the same clearness of poetical expression, although the poet speaks about things which are by their very nature unclear, unprecise, quavery, and nebulous. There is not the slightest pretension in the choice of words. . . There is the same iron logic as before in the unfolding of the lyrical thought, in the placement of 'proofs,' in the joining together of 'premises' and 'deductions'. . . The master did not tire, did not age, did not waste her substance, notwithstanding the many years of secluded life. On the contrary, in some ways she consolidated the foundations of her youth and began to write better." [48]

And, indeed, all this is demonstrated in such a fine and compact poem as this:

The Muse

When nightly I await her silent coming,
Life, seemingly, hangs on a single hair.
What's freedom, youth, and honors so becoming,
Before my guest with flute and features fair?

She entered. Throwing off her azure mantle
She looked at me and waited for my bid.
I asked of her: "Did you dictate to Dante
The stark *Inferno?*" She replied: "I did."

On the whole, Akhmatova's emotions are more controlled now and the ideological content is deeper than before. She is more sure of herself and of her medium. But there is a note of nostalgia which appears here and there, as in a remarkable poem about Lot's wife, who "gave her life for one look." And, no doubt, Akhmatova herself would gladly give her life for one look at that past which was life to her. But she who wrote

At baptism they gave me the name of Anna—
The sweetest for men's lips and hearing

will not suffer the fate of Lot's wife, but rather that of Niobe. Whatever her fate, she occupies already an important place on the Russian literary Olympus. Pre-revolutionary and post-revolutionary critics alike praise her. Zhirmunsky wrote in 1916: "Akhmatova is not only the most brilliant representative of the younger generation of poets, but she is endowed with traits that are eternal and traits that are individual, traits which do not fit completely into the temporary and the historical peculiarities of today's poetry."[49] This was echoed by Nedobrovo, who said: "All of us see approximately the same kind of people and yet after reading Akhmatova's poems we are filled with a new pride in life and in man."[50] And writing in the Soviet Literary Encyclopedia, S. Malakhov and P. Sakulin say: "In the person of Akhmatova we have a poet with an extremely strong talent."[51] One may also quote the sensitive and intelligent critic, Yuli Aikhenvald: ."Anna Akhmatova— the last flower of the noble Russian culture, the guardian of poetical piety, an embodiment of the past that is capable of consoling in the present and of providing hope for the future— belongs to spiritual Russia of all times."[52]

And as a corollary to these opinions there are no better words than those written by Leonid Grossman in 1924:

Akhmatova is the embodiment of the sorrowful thought about the life of the spirit uncured by the enchanted contemplation of the concrete loveliness of living forms. She represents also the clear, perspicacious, and loving reflection of the world, permeated by the hopeless perception of human fate. And this simple combination of two great moments of existence is blended into one of the most moving and finished manifestations of art.

That is why we are so charmed by these slim volumes of verse. That is why we are so taken by this vision of the world so definitely plastic in the reflection of its concrete forms, so genuinely tragic in its artistic treatment. That is why in the pleiad of Russian poetesses, to Anna Akhmatova immortally belongs the first place.[53]

During World War II, Anna Akhmatova's poetry appeared in the leading journals of the Soviet Union: in Leningrad in the monthlies *Krasnaya Nov'* (Red Virgin Soil), *Zvezda* (The

Star) and *Leningrad;* and in Moscow in the monthly *Znamya* (The Banner) and in the weekly *Ogonyok* (The Little Flame), the latter being the Soviet equivalent of our widely popular *Life.* Of these poems, some (obviously written for the occasion) are almost trite, as the following, written during the siege of Leningrad:

> And the one who today says good-bye to her lover
> Should her pain into strength, into courage reforge.
> And we swear to our children, to our dead left uncovered,
> That nothing will make us submit to brute force.

On the other hand, there are some as remarkable as the best that Akhmatova has ever written, as this terse poem about the craft of the poet, which, one may suggest, should not be read aloud, but rather in a hoarse whisper:

> Our sacred, hallowed craft
> Has existed thousands of years,
> Lighting the world with its blazing shaft;
> But no poet has said that there are no tears,
> That there is no wisdom or old-age fears,
> And even no death with its black-draped biers.

In 1942 Alexei N. Tolstoy called Akhmatova's latest poems "a high humanitarian art,"[54] and in 1943 her poems (both pre- and post-revolutionary) were included in an anthology published by the Literary Division of the State Publishing House (*Goslitizdat*), which contained also some poems of such pre-revolutionary writers as Blok, Bryusov, and Bely. Finally, on November 24, 1945, the official publication of the Governing Board of the Union of Soviet Writers, *Literaturnaya Gazeta* (The Literary Gazette), published an interview with Anna

Akhmatova accompanied by her photograph. In it the poetess said:

A large collection of my lyric poems (1909-1945), comprising about four thousand lines, is scheduled to be published early in 1946 by the Literary Division of the State Publishing House in Leningrad.*

In this collection my poems will be placed for the first time in strictly chronological order. My former books (*Evening, Rosary, White Flock,* etc.) will form separate parts of the collection. The last part is called Odd Number. It comprises my poems of the war years, mostly those dedicated to Leningrad, and a small cycle entitled The Moon in Ascendance, which I consider to be a series of sketches for a long poem about Central Asia, where I spent two and a half years and with which I have not yet parted creatively.

At present I am collecting and putting in order my essays about Pushkin (1926-1936). There are twenty-five of them and their content varies considerably. Among them there is one about Pushkin's self-repetition, another about his epistolary style, a third about his use of color epithets. Taken as a whole, these essays, observations, and notes form a book about Pushkin.

I am also continuing to work on my long poem *Triptich,* which was begun in 1940 and completed in a rough draft in 1942. This piece is composed of three parts: The Year 1913, Tail† (Intermezzo), and Epilogue.

I shall certainly continue to write lyric poetry also. But it is most difficult to speak about one's future lyric poems, because they get created by themselves, so to speak. . . I can only say that I am planning a cycle to be called Leningrad Elegies.

The publication of this interview was followed by a series of recitals of Akhmatova's poetry in Moscow, sponsored by

---

*It was never published.
†The reverse side of a coin.

the Union of Soviet Writers, which gathered large audiences and became a real triumph for her.

Anna Akhmatova—the poetess of tragic love—has stirred the hearts of readers of Russian poetry for thirty-five years and she is still writing, but again not publishing, because she encountered the wrath of the leaders of the Soviet Union. In a decree of the Central Committee of the All-Union Communist Party of Bolsheviks dated August 14, 1946, her poetry was condemned in the following words: "Akhmatova is a typical representative of empty poetry lacking in ideas and alien to our people. Her poems, permeated with the spirit of pessimism and decadence and expressing the tastes of old 'salon' poetry, which grew out of the position of burgeois-aristocratic aestheticism of 'art for art's sake' and which does not desire to keep in step with the people, do harm to the work of educating our youth and cannot be suffered in Soviet literature."[55] This was followed by her expulsion from the Union of Soviet Writers on September 4, 1946.[56] Although Akhmatova's voice has been silenced again, perhaps permanently, what she has said so far not only places her ahead of all living Russian poets, but assures for her a preëminent place in Russian poetry of all time as the greatest woman-poet the Russian nation has produced.

CHAPTER THREE

MANDELSTAM

Oh! sky, Oh! sky, about you I'll be dreaming!
It could not be that you're so diaphane.
Like a white page on fire the day was gleaming:
A little smoke and ash are all that now remain.
—Mandelstam, *Kamen'*

OSIP MANDELSTAM

Architect of the Word

In the early autumn of 1910 at the Warsaw railroad station in St. Petersburg a young man alighted from a third-class carriage of a train coming from Germany. No one met him; he had no luggage, having lost his only suitcase at the frontier. This traveler was dressed peculiarly. An Alpine hat on his head, a wide shabby cloak on his sloping shoulders, bright russet shoes in need of polish and well worn at the heels—such was his attire. Over his left arm a checkered steamer rug was draped and in his right hand he held a sandwich. Thus, sandwich in hand, he made his way to the exit. His name was Osip Emilyevich Mandelstam and he was to become the only Jewish member of the Acmeist clan. "In the suitcase lost at Eidtkunen there was, besides a toothbrush and a volume of Bergson, a much used notebook the pages of which were covered with verses. But the loss (except for the toothbrush) was not important because Mandelstam knew his verses and Bergson by heart."[1]

The son of an unsuccessful middle-class businessman, with whom failure followed upon failure, Mandelstam was born in Warsaw on January 15, 1891.[2] As a child he was brought to St. Petersburg and he grew up in that city. He did not enjoy a happy family life. After completing his secondary education in the Tenishev private school in 1907, he went abroad and spent some time in Paris. At that time he was much attracted by the poetry of Baudelaire and Verlaine. In 1910 he went abroad again and spent two terms at the University of Heidelberg in Germany studying Kantian philosophy and Old French. Upon his return to Russia he entered the University of St. Petersburg and joined the literary circles of the capital. From then on his unprepossessing figure was seen more often in bohemian cafes and restaurants, in the editorial rooms of reviews and at literary gatherings, than in the hallowed halls and auditoriums of the great seat of learning which was then the University of St. Petersburg.

Mandelstam presented an almost grotesque appearance. His thin, feeble body (always dressed in loud checkered suits) was surmounted by an unnaturally large head on a skinny neck. His reddish hair stood straight up surrounding a considerable baldness and his small bird-like face was framed by sideburns. He reminded one of a young cock. But his eyes, though framed by red-rimmed eyelids without eye-lashes, were shining, penetrating, beautiful eyes. And when he recited his poetry he became transfigured so that one forgot completely his ludicrous appearance. "Mandelstam was restless, bustling; he could not talk about anything consecutively for more than three minutes; he sat at the edge of a chair, all the time ready to run away somewhere as an engine under steam. But his verses are immovable; they possess that beauty which, according to Baudelaire, abhors even the slightest movement."[3]

Mandelstam's first verse which attracted much attention appeared in the July-August 1910 issue of *Apollon*.[4] "These poems were astonishing. Indeed, astonishing . . . When I read them," writes Georgi Ivanov, "I felt a knocking at my heart: 'Why did I not write them?' Such envy is a very characteristic feeling. Gumilyov considered that it evaluates 'the weight' of poetry more accurately than any analysis. If one has the feeling 'Why not I?'—you may be sure that the poetry is 'genuine.' "[5]

From 1910 on, most of Mandelstam's poetry appeared in the review *Apollon* and in the almanac published by that review.[6] In 1912 Mandelstam joined the Acmeist group, and in 1913 his first book was published by the Guild of Poets. It was entitled *Kamen'* (Stone). In it Mandelstam, whom a critic called "a troublous poet,"[7] revealed himself a true Acmeist, treating the word delicately but firmly, fully the master of his medium. "Mandelstam's mastery of words makes him akin to Tyutchev,"[8] one of the finest Russian poets of the nineteenth century. The poetry of Mandelstam is characterized "by an attraction for classical examples, by a grandiloquent severity, by the cult of historical themes,"[9] but primarily by a balancing fusion of the outer and inner worlds expressed in swaying rhythms. There is a feeling of permanency in his lines even beyond living existence and a contempt for the momentary, the transitional, that which is today and gone tomorrow. And he paid particular attention to craftsmanship. To him even beauty was man-made when he said:

> The beautiful's not a demi-god's whim
> But a simple carpenter's rapacious eye-measure.

In a greater way probably than with the other Acmeists, Mandelstam was fit to be a member of the Guild of Poets in its original, medieval sense because poetry to him was not only a calling but also a craft, as he showed it in this chiseled poem:

> A body's given me—what then to do with it,
> When it is so my own, so very definite?
>
> Whom should I thank, Oh! tell me, for the bliss,
> The quiet bliss to live and breathe like this?

87

I am the gardener and the bloom as well,
In nature's prison I do not rebel.

My breathing and my warmth have been impressed
Upon the windows of unendingness.

Their pattern will be set in rigid rhymes,
Unrecognizable from recent times.

And let the moment's turbidness flow down—
The lovely pattern's lines it could not drown.

Although at first Mandelstam seems to be introspective, in reality he is impersonal. The "I" in his poetry may not be Mandelstam at all, but merely a reflection of himself as provided by his imagination. Even his emotionalism seems detached:

Thy image, wavering, tormenting,
I could not in the fog discern.
"Oh, Lord!" I cried, my slip lamenting,
Not thinking in my deep concern.

God's name, its wings unfurling holy,
Flew out of my oppressed breast.
In front—thick fog is rolling slowly,
Behind—an empty cage unblest.

This impersonal quality of Mandelstam's poetry was commented upon by both pre- and post-revolutionary critics. Zhirmunsky, who considered Mandelstam next to Akhmatova the most interesting representative of the young poetry of the time, wrote: "Using the terminology of Friedrich Schlegel, one may call his verse not a poetry of life, but a poetry of poetry (*die Poesie der Poesie*); i.e., a poetry which has as its subject not life itself as perceived directly by the poet, but someone else's artistic conception of life."[10] And the Soviet critic Selivanovsky echoed this when he said: "Mandelstam's poetry is not a direct reflection of life, but a reflection of its reflection in art."[11] To this he added: "When we re-read the works of Mandelstam, it becomes clear to us that this poet is very much afraid of life, of real people, and of their real conflicts and experiences, and that he obtains relative peace only when from living people he turns to books. The most frightening thing for Mandelstam is any kind of change in reality. His demand for 'stability' in life and in art is nothing but a demand for their immobility and inertia. He has no social instincts or interests and he says himself: 'No, never was I a contemporary of anyone.'"[12]

There may be a good deal of truth in this, because in real life Mandelstam was afraid of everything and everybody.[13] But this timidity was only the timidity before the unknown. What Mandelstam knew he was not afraid of. And he knew poetry, he knew art. At times he even knew man, when he wrote in blank verse:

> Let names of flowering towns and cities
> Caress the ear by their fragile importance.
> It isn't Rome that lives throughout the ages,
> But man's location in the universe.
>
> Kings try to make him their possession,
> Priests justify the furthering of wars,
> Yet without him the houses, temples—
> Like piteous dust—are worthy of contempt.

Mandelstam loved "heavy," ponderous words. There is an architectural quality in his poetry. He said himself: "We do not fly, we merely ascend those towers which we can build

89

ourselves."[14] And he builds his poems, as once were built the Gothic towers of his beloved Notre Dame of Paris, of permanent material to last for ages. That is why the title of his first book, *Kamen'* (Stone), is so significant. But the choice of his material imposed upon the poet, the creator, the architect, its own limitations; hence there is "an imprint upon his poetry of artistic laconicism,"[15] which gives it a classical form.[16] This tendency toward classicism also forced Mandelstam to remain within the framework of the established rules of Russian prosody. Therefore, the often startling effects of his poetry are achieved solely by his style and the inner content of his poems, and not by any innovations of poetical form.

Like Akhmatova, he is epigrammatic in the recording of his impressions. But he does not prompt the reader by word-suggestions to perceive the mood of the picture he presents; on the contrary, he gives a precise and peculiar word formula of it.

It is interesting to examine closely how Mandelstam selects those particularities and details with which he re-creates the impression of this or that artistic presentation. Least of all can one call him an impressionist who reproduces directly and without selectivity, without any rational associations, those visual spots which are the first and as yet unrealized impressions of outer objects. At first glance the details consciously selected according to his artistic taste may seem accidental and unnoticeable; their meaning in the creative imagination of the poet is immeasurably exaggerated; a small item grows to fantastic proportions as if in a purposely distorted grotesqueness; at the same time the relation in perspective between insignificant and large objects disappears; the distant and the near-by in the projection on the surface appear of equal dimensions. But in this deliberate distortion and fantastic exaggeration a previously unnoticed particularity becomes expressive and characteristic of the subject under presentation.[17]

When reviewing the second enlarged edition of Mandelstam's *Kamen'* Gumilyov wrote: "The poet becomes an adept of the literary movement known under the name of Acmeism. He has used to perfection the knowledge that not a single image has an independent meaning and is needed only for the purpose of revealing the poet's soul as fully as possible."[18]

Since his days at Heidelberg, Mandelstam had been interested in philosophy, which he continued to study while a student at the University of St. Petersburg. In 1913 he was particularly attracted by Roman Catholic universalism and by the pro-Catholic Russian philosopher of the first part of the nineteenth century, Peter Chaadayev, about whom he later wrote an article in *Apollon*.[19] Also in 1913 he wrote an article on François Villon, which was accompanied by Gumilyov's translations from Villon's works.[20] The next year his interest shifted to the Christian philosopher Constantine Leontiev.[21]

During World War I the poetry of Mandelstam, unlike that of his master Gumilyov, did not reflect any war themes with the exception of one remarkable piece, written in 1916 and entitled "Menagerie." Beginning with the lines

> The word of peace has been rejected
> At the beginning of our offended era,

it tells how while the world was busy with its peaceful pursuits, "the German raised an eagle," "the lion submitted to the Briton," "the Gallic cock grew a comb as a weapon," and the savage took hold of the earth. The poet then proposes to build a cage and to place therein "the cock, the lion, the eagle, and the bear," and having secured the beasts in their menagerie

> We shall then have acquired peace for long;
> And then the Volga's waters will be fuller,
> The Rhine's bright stream will sing a song.

On the whole, as a poet Mandelstam is not a realist as some of the other Acmeists were (Gorodetsky, Narbut, Zenkevich), nor even a romantic realist as Gumilyov was. He is more of a fanciful realist in the fashion of E. T. Hoffmann. According to his poetical technique he could be called a fantastic creator of words in the same manner in which the German poet could be called a fantastic creator of images and plots. Nevertheless, Mandelstam has a kinship with his generation of Russian poets "in the absence of the personal, emotional, and mystical elements in their poetical presentation as well as in their conscious word technique, their love for graphic detail, and their consummate epigrammatic treatment of expression."[22]

When the first revolution occurred in 1917, Mandelstam did not choose to follow the new paths, although in his youth he belonged at one time to the Socialist-Revolutionary Party and was active in socialist propaganda among the workers of St. Petersburg.[23] "The October [November] revolution did not produce any upheavals in Mandelstam's poetical creation,"[24] but his poetry now reveals pessimism and resignation. He defines the state of affairs in one line: "From easy life we lost our mind." There is not much left now to do:

> Only children's books to read,
> Only children's thoughts to cherish,
> All that's great to cast adrift,
> And from endless grief to perish.

In 1918 he wrote a deep and penetrating poem entitled "The Dusk of Freedom":

> Let's, brethren, glorify the dusk of freedom,
> The great and dusky year.
>
> . . .

Let's glorify the dusky weight of power
And its intolerable yoke.
Who has a heart must hear, oh! timeless hour,
How your ship sinks in smoke.

. . .

Well, let us try this huge, unwieldy
And screechy rudder's turn.

. . .

We shall remember when to Lethe yielding
That heaven we must earn.

Commenting on this poem, Ilya Ehrenburg wrote: "Poets greeted the Russian revolution by wild exclamations, by the tears and cries of the possessed by the devil, by ecstatic delirium, by curses. But Mandelstam—the poor Mandelstam who never drinks unboiled water and who crosses the street when he has to pass by a police station—was the only one to comprehend the pathos of events. The 'great men' vociferated, but the little busybody of the St. Petersburg cafes, having understood the grand scale of what was happening, the majesty of history in the making, glorified the madness of our times when he exclaimed: 'Well, let us try this huge, unwieldy and screechy rudder's turn.' "[25] But although Mandelstam was willing to assist the "rudder's turn" of the Russian ship of state it proved eventually his undoing both as poet and as man.

In the same year he wrote a beautiful, haunting poem about the city in which he was raised and came to maturity, the city he loved so much—St. Petersburg—Petrograd—Petropolis:

On fearful heights—an erring light.
But is it thus a star is hieing?
Translucent star, the erring light,
Your kin, Petropolis, is dying.

93

On fearful heights burn earthly dreams;
An emerald star is slowly flying.
If you are sky's and water's kin,
Your kin, Petropolis, is dying.

A monstrous ship on fearful heights
Unfurls its wings all space defying.
Oh, emerald star! In great distress
Your kin, Petropolis, is dying.

Translucent spring o'er Neva's night
Broke down. Eternity is crying.
If you're Petropolis, oh, star,
Your town, Petropolis, is dying.

This heart-rending cry of distress from the very soul of a poet who wrote hitherto such impersonal and impassionate poetry is very significant. As his world went crumbling down around him, he could not fail to be moved. But soon thereafter comes a note of profound resignation:

All that is here was once before and will occur again,
And sweet to us is but the moment of cognition.

The poet "deliberately denies the novelty of what is happening about him," in the words of the Soviet critic A. Tarasenkov,[26] and turns his back to the present.

All these poems written since 1914 appeared in Mandelstam's second book, characteristically entitled *Tristia* and published in 1922.[27] This book contained also a beautifully worded poem in blank verse:

Take for your joy from my outstretched palms
A little bit of sun, a little bit of honey,
As bees tell us Persephone has ordered.

94

One can't unfasten an unfastened boat,
One cannot hear the furry steps of shadows,
One cannot master fear in this primeval life.

All that is left to us are only kisses
Like shaggy tiny bees that promptly die
As soon as they have left the beehive's safety.

Take then for joy my reckless, crazy present—
A dry unsightly necklace made of bees
Who died while into sunshine changing honey.

Although from these poems it is obvious that Mandelstam was out of tune with what was happening in Soviet Russia, he remained there, as did Gumilyov and Akhmatova. For a while, after the death of Gumilyov, he tried to head a movement for the establishment of a new classicism in Russian poetry[28] which coincided with a general revival of interest among Soviet poets in Pushkin and his contemporaries. But the revolutionary tempo of spreading materialism, the accent on proletarian literature, and the hostile attitude of Soviet critics prevented the development of the movement. Less and less frequently could one hear the poet's voice, which sounded rarely even in normal times. In 1923 he published a long poem in free verse (the first in this form for Mandelstam) called "The Finder of a Horseshoe", in which he "proclaimed the principle of inertia as belonging to a 'primevally eternal' category".[29] Two years later he published a remarkable poem reminiscent of Gumilyov's "The Trolley Car Which Lost Its Way" and written in 1921, the same year in which Gumilyov's poem was composed. It was entitled "A Concert in a Railway Station." In it Mandelstam compares the noises of steam and the clank of metal to the music of an orchestra. But into the reality of a railway station enters the fantasy of the poet who speaks of "cars departing to Elysian fields" and of others solidly entrenched in the present. "I missed the train. I'm frightened. It's a dream," exclaims the poet and concludes his poem with these sad lines:

> Why all this rush? At funeral's repast for our
>   beloved ghost
> For the last time the music plays for us.

Commenting on this poem the Soviet critic, G. Lelevich, wrote: "The principal thing in it is an obvious feeling of the crumbling of the world of reality, a feeling of having reached a fearful boundary, a limit, beyond which begins the agony, the realization of the nearness of the end."[30] This Marxist critic was probably right, for in 1925 Mandelstam stopped writing poetry and turned to prose.[31] He published first a collection of autobiographical sketches, *Shum Vremeni* (The Noise of Time), and later a most interesting novelette entitled *Yegipetskaya Marka* (The Egyptian Stamp). From then on, he devoted most of his time to translations.

In 1928, however, he published a collection of his poetical works embracing, in 190 pages, practically everything he had written in his lifetime as a poet. It was composed of an almost complete reprint of his books *Kamen'* and *Tristia* and of a third section which comprised poems written between 1921 and 1925. All of the poems were placed in strict chronological order according to the year of composition. For reasons of his own, Mandelstam deleted four poems from *Kamen'* and added five, which had not appeared in the revised edition of 1923. In *Tristia* he added two poems not found in the edition of 1921, but deleted twelve, including "The Dusk of Freedom" and "Petropolis," these for obvious political reasons.

The last section opened with "A Concert in a Railway Station" and included "The Finder of a Horseshoe," which was published in the 1923 edition of *Kamen'*. The remaining eighteen pieces repeat the poet's disenchantment with his surroundings, his aloofness from the present, and his longing for the past. These feelings are most graphically expressed in a poem "This Age," dated 1923. In it Mandelstam compares the age he is living in to a wild animal who is mortally wounded, but who strives nevertheless to reach his appointed goal. Yet it is all in vain, since time has already sacrificed him as it did the lamb of yore. And the poet ends his lament saying:

> But your spine is sadly broken
> Oh, my lovely piteous age.
>
> With a smile inane and senseless
> You, malign yet weak, look back,
> Like a beast once young and supple,
> On your paws' own-fashioned track.

After 1928 Mandelstam's name disappeared from the roster of writers in the Soviet Union. Death finally came to him, then an obscure translator, in 1945. But as a poet, Mandelstam died twenty years before that, when at the funeral repast for his beloved ghost, music of divine inspiration played for him for the last time. "Mandelstam's place as one of the most outstanding poets of our time is firmly established and generally recognized. The high art of the word, linked as it is with an 'instinctive restraint of speech,' gives his poems a unique and exclusive charm."[32]

Together with Gumilyov and Akhmatova, he forms the immortal trinity on the poetical Olympus of Russia's literary renaissance of the twentieth century.

Notes

NOTES

INTRODUCTION

1. Valery Bryusov, "Sud akmeista," *Pechat' i Revolyutsiya*, 1923, No. 2, p. 87.
2. A. Volkov, *Poeziya Russkogo Imperializma* (Moscow, 1935), p. 48.
3. B. Eikhenbaum, *Anna Akhmatova* (Petersburg, 1923), p. 66.
4. "Postanovlenie TsK VKP(b) ot 14 avgusta 1946 g.," *Znamya (Organ Soyuza Sovetskikh Pisatelei SSSR)*, 1946, No. 10, p. 5.
5. "Vyshe znamya ideinosti v literature!" *ibid.*, p. 34.
6. Volkov, *Poeziya*, p. 160.
7. Innokenty Oksyonov, "Sovetskaya poeziya i nasledie akmeizma," *Literaturny Leningrad*, 1934, No. 24.
8. Nikolai Stepanov, "Poeticheskoe nasledie akmeizma," *ibid.*, No. 35.

CHAPTER ONE · NICHOLAS GUMILYOV

1. B. Koz'min, *Pisateli Sovremennoi Epokhi*, I (Moscow, 1928), 109.
2. Mikhail Struve, "N. S. Gumilyovu," *Russkaya Mysl'*, 1921, Nos. 10-12, p. 87.
3. G. Lelevich, "Gumilyov, N. S.," *Bol'shaya Sovetskaya Entsiklopediya*.
4. Valery Bryusov, "Sud akmeista," *Pechat' i Revolyutsiya*, 1923, No. 2, p. 98.
5. Pyotr Struve, "In Memoriam," *Russkaya Mysl'*, 1921, Nos. 10-12, p. 91.

6. Georgi Ivanov, Preface to Nicholas Gumilyov, *Stikhotvoreniya, Posmertny Sbornik* (2nd ed., Petrograd, 1923), p. 6.
7. Koz'min, *Pisateli*, p. 109.
8. Nicholas Gumilyov, "Pis'ma o russkoi poezii," *Apollon*, 1910, No. 8, p. 59.
9. Nicholas Gumilyov, "Zhizn' stikha," *Apollon*, 1910, No. 7, p. 16.
10. Lelevich, "Gumilyov," *B. S. E.*, quoting Zhirmunsky.
11. *Ibid.*
12. Quoted in A. Volkov, *Poeziya Russkogo Imperializma* (Moscow, 1935), p. 125.
13. *Ibid.*, pp. 125-126.
14. *Vesy*, 1905, No. 11, p. 68.
15. Koz'min, *Pisateli*, p. 26.
16. Lelevich, "Gumilyov," *B. S. E.*
17. Georgi Ivanov, Preface to Nicholas Gumilyov, *Chuzhoe Nebo* (2nd ed., Berlin, 1936), p. 4.
18. *Apollon*, 1914, Nos. 1-2, p. 135.
19. Innokenty Annensky, "O sovremennom lirizme," *Apollon*, 1909, No. 2, p. 25.
20. Bryusov, "Sud akmeista," pp. 96-100.
21. Gumilyov, "Pis'ma," *Apollon*, 1911, No. 10, p. 74; 1910, No. 5, p. 56; 1912, No. 1, p. 72; 1915, No. 10, p. 51; 1910, No. 9, p. 38; 1912, No. 6, p. 54.
22. *Ibid.*, 1914, No. 5, p. 35; 1912, No. 6, p. 54; 1914, No. 5, p. 35.
23. Gumilyov, "Zhizn' stikha," p. 6.
24. Gumilyov, "Pis'ma," *Apollon*, 1911, No. 5, p. 76; 1912, No. 5, p. 50.
25. *Ibid.*, 1912, No. 8, p. 60.
26. *Ibid.*, 1912, No. 6, pp. 52-53.
27. Gumilyov, "Zhizn' stikha," p. 7.
28. Gumilyov, "Pis'ma," *Apollon*, 1910, No. 9, p. 36; 1910, No. 10, p. 25; 1915, No. 10, p. 52.
29. *Ibid.*, 1910, No. 8, p. 61.
30. Gumilyov, "Zhizn' stikha," pp. 8-9.
31. *Apollon*, 1910, No. 7, p. 38.
32. Gumilyov, "Pis'ma," *Apollon*, 1913, No. 3, p. 75.
33. Volkov, *Poeziya*, p. 123.
34. V. Dynnik, "Akmeizm," *B. S. E.*
35. Koz'min, *Pisateli*, p. 110.
36. Valery Bryusov, "Antologiya izd. Musaget," *Russkaya Mysl'*, 1911, No. 8, p. 15.

37. Valery Bryusov, *Dalyokie i Blizkie* (1911), quoted in Volkov, *Poeziya*, p. 116.
38. Mikhail Kuzmin, "Pis'ma o russkoi poezii," *Apollon*, 1912, No. 2, p. 74.
39. Volkov, *Poeziya*, p. 133; Lelevich, "Gumilyov," *B. S. E.*
40. Lelevich, "Gumilyov," *B. S. E.*
41. Volkov, *Poeziya*, p. 115.
42. Gleb Struve, "Pis'ma o russkoi poezii," *Russkaya Mysl'*, 1922, Nos. 6-7, p. 240.
43. E. Anichkov, *Novaya Russkaya Poeziya* (Berlin, 1921), p. 108; V. Zhirmunsky, "Preodolevshie simvolizm," *Russkaya Mysl'*, 1916, No. 12, p. 49.
44. Bryusov, "Sud akmeista," p. 87.
45. Volkov, *Poeziya*, p. 117.
46. Gumilyov, "Nasledie simvolizma i akmeizm," *Apollon*, 1913, No. 1, pp. 42-45.
47. Sergei Gorodetsky, "Nekotorye techeniya v sovremennoi russkoi poezii," *Apollon*, 1913, No. 1, pp. 49-50.
48. Volkov, *Poeziya*, pp. 115-116.
49. Valery Bryusov, "Novyya techeniya v russkoi poezii, Akmeizm," *Russkaya Mysl'*, 1913, No. 4, pp. 134-142.
50. Dynnik, "Akmeizm," *B. S. E.*
51. Georgi Ivanov, Preface to Gumilyov, *Pis'ma o Russkoi Poezii* (Petrograd, 1923) p. 8.
52. *Apollon*, 1913, No. 1, p. 70.
53. *Ibid.*, 1914, Nos. 1-2, p. 135; 1914, No. 5, p. 54.
54. *Ibid.*, 1911, No. 9, pp. 59-64; 1913, No. 4, pp. 36-38.
55. Andrei Levinson, "Gumilyov," *Sovremennyya Zapiski*, IX (1922), 311.
56. *Apollon*, 1914, No. 5, p. 54.
57. Volkov, *Poeziya*, p. 207.
58. Pyotr Struve, "In Memoriam," p. 91.
59. Gumilyov, "Pis'ma," *Apollon*, 1909, No. 2, p. 21.
60. *Posluzhnoi Spisok Praporshchika 5 Gusarskago Aleksandriyskago Yeya Velichestva Gosudaryni Imperatritsy Aleksandry Fyodorovny polka Gumilyova*, p. 3.
61. Georgi Ivanov, "Voyennye stikhi," *Apollon*, 1915, Nos. 4-5, p. 84.
62. Translated by Gerald Shelley in *Modern Poems from Russia* (London, 1942).
63. Volkov, *Poeziya*, p. 187. *Birzhevye Vedomosti* is not available in the United States.

64. *Apollon*, 1916, No. 2, p. 55; 1916, Nos. 4-5, p. 86.
65. Zhirmunsky, "Preodolevshie," p. 51.
66. Ivanov, Preface to *Chuzhoe Nebo*, p. 7.
67. Translated by Gerald Shelley.
68. M. Tumpovskaya, " 'Kolchan,' N. Gumilyova," *Apollon*, 1917, Nos. 6-7, pp. 58-69; Zhirmunsky, "Preodolevshie," pp. 49-52.
69. B. Eikhenbaum, "Novye stikhi N. Gumilyova," *Russkaya Mysl'*, 1916, No. 2, pp. 17-19; Zhirmunsky, "Preodolevshie," p. 52.
70. For obvious reasons the second quotation was omitted by the publishers from the Berlin edition.
71. Volkov, *Poeziya*, pp. 207-208.
72. Lelevich, "Gumilyov," *B. S. E.*
73. Leonid Chatsky (Strakhovsky), "N. Goumilev," *Russian Life*, 1921, Nos. 2-3, p. 72.
74. Ivanov, Preface to Gumilyov, *Pis'ma*, p. 7.
75. *Apollon*, 1916, No. 1, pp. 13-15.
76. Lelevich, "Gumilyov," *B. S. E.*
77. This and sixteen other poems of *Kostyor* were reprinted in *Russkaya Mysl'*, 1922, Nos. 1-2, pp. 3-17.
78. *Petrogradskaya Pravda*, September 1, 1921. p. 1.
79. Volkov, *Poeziya*, p. 212.
80. V. F. Khodasevich, *Nekropol'. Vospominaniya* (Bruxelles, 1939), pp. 122-123.
81. Gleb Struve, "Pis'ma," p. 240.
82. *Ibid.*, p. 246.
83. Lelevich, "Gumilyov," *B. S. E.*
84. Gleb Struve, "Blok and Gumilyov," *The Slavonic and East European Review*, XXV, No. 64 (November 1946), 179.
85. *Kniga i Revolyutsiya*, 1921, No. 1 (13), p. 31.
86. Koz'min, *Pisateli*, p. 110. There is considerable uncertainty as to the actual date of Gumilyov's death. While Koz'min gives the date of August 25, I. V. Vladislavlev (*Literatura Velikogo Desyatiletiya*, I [Moscow-Leningrad, 1928], 90) has August 24. On the other hand, both Georgi Ivanov ("O Gumilyove," *Sovremennya Zapiski*, XLVII [1931], p. 308) and Khodasevich (*Nekropol'*, p. 118) give the date of August 27.
87. He was actually thirty-five. Georgi Ivanov is also in error when he gives his age as forty (Preface to *Chuzhoe Nebo*, p. 3).
88. *Petrogradskaya Pravda*, September 1, 1921, p. 1.
89. Ivanov, Preface to *Chuzhoe Nebo*, pp. 3-4.
90. *Ibid.*, pp. 5-7.

1. Translated by Gerald Shelley in *Modern Poems from Russia* (London, 1942); slightly revised.
2. Georgi Ivanov, *Peterburgskiya Zimy* (Paris, 1928), p. 67.
3. Leonid Grossman, "Anna Akhmatova," *Mastera Slova* (Moscow, 1928), pp. 303-304.
4. Valerian Chudovsky, "Po povodu stikhov Anny Akhmatovoi," *Apollon*, 1912, No. 5, pp. 45, 47; Grossman, *Mastera Slova*, p. 301.
5. Yuli Aikhenval'd, "Anna Akhmatova," *Siluety Russkikh Pisatelei* (Berlin, 1923), III, 279.
6. Translated by Shelley, revised.
7. V. L'vov-Rogachevsky, *Noveishaya Russkaya Literatura* (Moscow, 1927), p. 303.
8. K. Mochul'sky, "Poeticheskoe tvorchestvo Anny Akhmatovoi," *Russkaya Mysl'*, March-April 1921, p. 186.
9. V. Zhirmunsky, "Preodolevshie simvolism," *Russkaya Mysl'*, 1916, No. 12, p. 33.
10. *Literaturnaya Entsiklopediya*, I (Moscow-Leningrad, 1930), 280; I. V. Vladislavlev, *Literatura Velikogo Desyatiletiya*, I (Moscow-Leningrad, 1928), 39.
11. Ivanov, *Peterburgskiya*, p. 71.
12. B. Koz'min, *Pisateli Sovremennoi Epokhi*, I (Moscow, 1928), 26.
13. B. V. Mikhailovsky, *Russkaya Literatura XX Veka* (Moscow, 1939), p. 337.
14. N. V. Nedobrovo, "Anna Akhmatova," *Russkaya Mysl'*, July 1915, p. 55.
15. Leonid I. Strakhovsky, "Anna Akhmatova: The Sappho of Russia," *The Russian Student*, VI, No. 3 (November 1929), 8.
16. Grossman, *Mastera*, p. 305.
17. Zhirmunsky, "Preodolevshie," p. 34.
18. Grossman, *Mastera*, pp. 309-310.
19. Aikhenval'd, *Siluety*, III, 281.
20. This poem is dated 1913.
21. Translated by Shelley; slightly revised. This poem is dated January 1914.
22. Strakhovsky, "Akhmatova," p. 8.
23. Grossman, *Mastera*, p. 308.
24. Translated by Shelley; slightly revised.

25. Translated by Shelley, revised. This poem is dated January 1, 1913.
26. Translated by Shelley.
27. Translated by Shelley, slightly revised.
28. Aikhenval'd, *Siluety*, III, 282.
29. Mikhailovsky, *Russkaya*, p. 337.
30. L'vov-Rogachevsky, *Noveishaya*, p. 303.
31. Later in Akhmatova's poetry it was "the white color, most exactly rendering the compactness and impenetrability of material and at the same time encompassing a complex emotional content, which became Akhmatova's favorite epithet" (Mochul'sky, "Poeticheskoe," p. 187).
32. N. Gumilyov, "Pis'mo o russkoi poezii," *Apollon*, 1914, No. 5, pp. 36-38.
33. Aikhenval'd, *Siluety*, III, 285.
34. Anna Akhmatova, "U samogo morya," *Apollon*, 1915, No. 3, pp. 25-32. When published in book form in 1921 it bore an epigraph taken from an unpublished poem by Gumilyov:
    "The world is but the shadow of a friend's face
        And all the rest is but its shadow."
    It is also included in the fourth enlarged edition of *Belaya Staya* (Petersburg, 1923).
35. G. Lelevich, *Na Postu* (1923), quoted in *Literaturnaya Entsiklopediya*, I, 281.
36. Orest Tsekhnovitser, *Literatura i Mirovaya Voina* (Moscow, 1938), p. 279.
37. *Literaturnaya Entsiklopediya*, I, 282, quoting *Belaya Staya*.
38. Translated by Shelley. This poem is dated 1915.
39. This poem is dated 1916.
40. This poem is dated 1917.
41. Mikhailovsky, *Russkaya*, p. 335.
42. A. Selivanovsky, *Ocherki po Istorii Russkoi Sovetskoi Poezii* (Moscow, 1936), p. 59.
43. Ivanov, *Peterburgskiya*, p. 74.
44. *Ibid.*
45. *Kniga i Revolyutsiya*, 1922, No. 3 (15), p. 72.
46. Gleb Struve, "Pisma o russkoi poezii," *Russkaya Mysl'*, 1922, Nos. 6-7, p. 242.
47. Ivanov, *Peterburgskiya*, pp. 64-65.
48. V. Pertsov, "Chitaya Akhmatovu," *Literaturnaya Gazeta*, July 10, 1940, No. 38 (889), p. 3.
49. Zhirmunsky, "Preodolevshie," p. 32.

50. Nedobrovo, "Akhmatova," p. 67.
51. *Literaturnaya Entsiklopediya*, I, 282.
52. Aikhenval'd, *Siluety*, III, 293.
53. Grossman, *Mastera*, p. 311.
54. A. Tolstoy, "O literature i voine," *Literatura i Iskusstvo*, December 5, 1942, No. 49.
55. "O zhurnalakh 'Zvezda' i 'Leningrad,'" *Znamya*, (*Organ Soyuza Sovetskikh Pisatelei SSSR*), October 1946, No. 10, p. 4.
56. "Rezolyutsiya Prezidiuma Pravleniya Soyuza Sovetskikh Pisatelei SSSR," *Oktyabr'* (*Organ Soyuza Sovetskikh Pisatelei SSSR*), 1946, No. 9, p. 187.

CHAPTER THREE · OSIP MANDELSTAM

1. Georgi Ivanov, *Peterburgskiya Zimy* (Paris, 1928), p. 108.
2. B. Koz'min, *Pisateli Sovremennoi Epokhi*, I (Moscow, 1928), 178; *Literaturnaya Entsiklopediya*, VI (Moscow-Leningrad, 1932), 756; I. V. Vladislavlev, *Literatura Velikogo Desyatiletiya*, I (Moscow-Leningrad, 1928), 83.
3. Ilya Ehrenburg, *Portrety Russkikh Poetov* (Berlin, 1922), p. 103.
4. *Apollon*, 1910, No. 9, pp. 5-7. Koz'min erroneously gives the date of 1909 (*Pisateli*, p. 178).
5. Ivanov, *Peterburgskiya*, p. 113.
6. *Al'manakh Apollon* (St. Petersburg, 1912), pp. 40-41.
7. E. Anichkov, *Novaya Russkaya Poeziya* (Berlin, 1921), p. 113.
8. K. Mochul'sky, "O. E. Mandel'shtam," *Vstrecha*, November 1945, p. 31.
9. *Literaturnaya Entsiklopediya*, VI, 757.
10. V. Zhirmunsky, "Preodolevshie simvolizm," *Russkaya Mysl'*, 1916, No. 12, pp. 43-44.
11. A. Selivanovsky, *Ocherki po Istorii Russkoi Sovetskoi Poezii* (Moscow, 1936), p. 60.
12. *Ibid.*
13. Ehrenburg, *Portrety*, p. 104; Ivanov, *Peterburgskiya*, p. 121.
14. Selivanovsky, *Ocherki*, p. 50.
15. *Literaturnaya Entsiklopediya*, VI, 757.

16. Mandelstam was very fond of French classicism and did excellent translations from Racine.
17. Zhirmunsky, "Preodolevshie," p. 46.
18. Nicholas Gumilyov, "Pis'ma o russkoi poezii," *Apollon*, 1916, No. 1, p. 31.
19. Osip Mandelstam, "Pyotr Chaadayev," *Apollon*, 1915, Nos. 6-7, pp. 57-62.
20. Osip Mandelstam, "François Villon," *Apollon*, 1913, No. 4, pp. 30-35.
21. Koz'min, *Pisateli*, p. 179.
22. Zhirmunsky, "Preodolevshie," p. 49.
23. Koz'min, *Pisateli*, p. 178.
24. *Literaturnaya Entsiklopediya*, VI, 757.
25. Ehrenburg, *Portrety*, pp. 104-105.
26. *Literaturnaya Entsiklopediya*, VI, 758.
27. Osip Mandelstam, *Tristia* (Petersburg-Berlin, 1922 [although the cover bears the date 1921]; 2nd ed., entitled *Vtoraya Kniga. Stikhi*, Moscow, 1923).
28. L'vov-Rogachevsky, *Noveishaya*, p. 303.
29. *Literaturnaya Entsiklopediya*, VI, 758.
30. G. Lelevich, "Gippokratovo litso," *Krasnaya Nov'*, 1925, No. 1, p. 297.
31. *Literaturnaya Entsiklopediya*, VI, 758.
32. Kn. D. Svyatopolk-Mirsky, "O. Mandel'shtam: Shum Vremeni," *Sovremennyya Zapiski*, XXV (1925), 541.

Bibliography

BIBLIOGRAPHY

Aikhenval'd, Yuli, *Siluety Russkikh Pisatelei*, vol. III (Berlin, 1923).
Akhmatova, Anna, *Anno Domini MCMXXI* (Petrograd, 1922; 2nd ed., 1923).
────── *Belaya Staya* (Petrograd, 1917; 4th enlarged ed., Petersburg, 1923).
────── "Budushchie Knigi," *Literaturnaya Gazeta*, November 24, 1945, No. 48.
────── *Chyotki* (St. Petersburg, 1914; 8th ed., Petersburg, 1922).
────── *Iz Shesti Knig* (Leningrad, 1940).
────── "Novye stikhi," *Znamya*, 1945, No. 4.
────── *Podorozhnik* (Petrograd, 1921).
────── "Stikhi," *Krasnaya Nov'*, 1942, Nos. 3-4.
────── "Stikhi raznykh let," *Zvezda*, 1946, No. 1.
────── *U Samogo Morya* (Petersburg, 1921).
────── *Vecher* (St. Petersburg, 1912).
Al'manakh Apollon (St. Petersburg, 1912).
Anichkov, E., *Novaya Russkaya Poeziya* (Berlin, 1921).
Annensky, Innokenty, "O sovremennom lirizme," *Apollon*, 1909, No. 2.
Bol'shaya Sovetskaya Entsiklopediya.
Bryusov, Valery, "Antologiya izd. Musaget," *Russkaya Mysl'*, 1911, No. 8.
────── "Novye sborniki stikhov," *Russkaya Mysl'*, February 1911.
────── "Novyya techeniya v russkoi poezii, Akmeizm," *Russkaya Mysl'*, 1913, No. 4.
────── "Sud akmeista," *Pechat' i Revolyutsiya*, 1923, No. 2.
Chatsky (Strakhovsky), Leonid, "N. Goumilev," *Russian Life*, 1921, Nos. 2-3.
Chudovsky, Valerian, "Po povodu stikhov Anny Akhmatovoi," *Apollon*, 1912, No. 5.

Ehrenburg, Ilya, *Portrety Russkikh Poetov* (Berlin, 1922).

Eikhenbaum, B., *Anna Akhmatova* (Petersburg, 1923).

—— "Novye stikhi N. Gumilyova," *Russkaya Mysl'*, 1916, No. 2.

Gorodetsky, Sergei, "Kamen' O. Mandel'shtama," *Rech'*, 1913, No. 162.

—— "Nekotorye techeniya v sovremennoi russkoi poezii," *Apollon*, 1913, No. 1.

Grossman, Leonid, *Mastera Slova* (Moscow, 1928).

Gumilyov, Nicholas, *Chuzhoe Nebo* (St. Petersburg, 1912; 2nd ed., with a preface by Georgi Ivanov, Berlin, 1936). The second edition (the only one available in the United States) is incomplete, lacking among others a play in verse, *Don Juan in Egypt*, and Gumilyov's translations from Théophile Gautier's *Emaux et Camées*.

—— *Ditya Allakha* (Petersburg, 1918; 2nd ed., Berlin, 1922). First published in *Apollon*, 1917, No. 6-7, pp. 17-57.

—— *Gondla* (Berlin, 1936). First published in *Russkaya Mysl'*, 1917, No. 1, pp. 67-97.

—— *Kolchan* (Petrograd, 1916; 2nd ed., Berlin, 1923).

—— *Kostyor* (Petersburg, 1918; 2nd ed., Berlin, 1922).

—— *K Sinei Zvezde* (Berlin, 1923).

—— *Mik Afrikanskaya Poema* (Petersburg, 1918; 2nd ed., Petrograd, 1922 [on title page, 1921]).

—— "Nasledie simvolizma i akmeism," *Apollon*, 1913, No. 1.

—— *Ognenny Stolp* (Petersburg, 1921; 2nd ed., Berlin, 1922).

—— *Pis'ma o Russkoi Poezii* (Petrograd, 1923).

—— *Put' Konkvistadorov* (St. Petersburg, 1905). Out of print and not available in the United States.

—— *Romanticheskie Tsvety* (Paris, 1908; 3rd ed., Petersburg, 1918).

—— *Shatyor* (Sevastopol, 1921; 2nd ed., Reval [Tallin], 1921; also Petersburg, 1921). The latter edition published by the Guild of Poets is incomplete.

—— *Stikhotvoreniya. Posmertny Sbornik*, with a preface by Georgi Ivanov (Petrograd, 1922; 2nd ed., 1923).

—— *Ten' ot Pal'my* (Petrograd, 1922).

—— *Zhemchuga* (Moscow, 1910; 2nd ed., Petersburg, 1918; 3rd ed., Berlin, 1921).

—— "Zhizn stikha," *Apollon*, 1910, No. 7.

—— tr., *Emali i Kamei* by Théophile Gautier (St. Petersburg, 1914). This book is not available in the United States.

—— tr., *Farforovy Pavil'on: Kitaiskie Stikhi* (Petrograd, 1918; 2nd ed., enlarged, Petrograd, 1922).

—— tr., *Frantsuzskie Narodnye Pesni* (Berlin, 1923).

—— tr., *Gil'gamesh. Vavilonsky Epos* (Petersburg, 1919).

—— tr., *Poema o Starom Moryake* by S. T. Coleridge (Petersburg, 1919).

—— in collaboration with K. Chukovsky and F. Batyushkov, *Printsipy Khudozhestvennogo Perevoda* (Petersburg, 1919).

Ivanov, Georgi, "Ispytanie ognyom," *Apollon*, 1914, No. 8.

—— "O Gumilyove," *Sovremennyya Zapiski*, vol. XLVII (1931).

—— *Peterburgskiya Zimy* (Paris, 1928).

—— "Voyennye stikhi," *Apollon*, 1915, Nos. 4-5.

Karenin, Dmitry, "Podlinny Gumilyov," *Posev*, No. 33 (82), 1947.

Khodasevich, V. F., *Nekropol'.Vospominaniya* (Bruxelles, 1939).

Kniga i Revolyutsiya, No. 1 (13), 1921; No. 3 (15), 1922.

Koz'min, B., *Pisateli Sovremmennoi Epokhi*, vol. I (Moscow, 1928).

Kuzmin, Mikhail, "Pis'ma o russkoi poezii," *Apollon*, 1912, No. 2.

Lelevich, G., "Gippokratovo litso," *Krasnaya Nov'*, 1925, No. 1.

Levinson, Andrei, "Gumilyov," *Sovremennyya Zapiski*, vol. IX (1922).

Literaturnaya Entsiklopediya.

L'vov-Rogachevsky, V., *Noveishaya Russkaya Literatura* (Moscow, 1927).

Mandelstam, Osip, "François Villon," *Apollon*, 1913, No. 4.

—— *Kamen'* (St. Petersburg, 1913; 2nd ed., Petrograd, 1916; 3rd ed., Moscow, 1923).

—— "Pyotr Chaadayev," *Apollon*, 1915, Nos. 6-7.

—— *Shum Vremeni* (Moscow, 1925).

—— *Stikhotvoreniya* (Moscow-Leningrad, 1928).

—— *Tristia* (Petersburg-Berlin, 1922 [the cover bears the date 1921]; 2nd ed., entitled *Vtoraya Kniga.Stikhi*, Moscow, 1923).

—— *Yegipetskaya Marka* (Leningrad, 1928). It contains also a reprint of *Shum Vremeni*.

Mikhailovsky, B. V., *Russkaya Literatura XX Veka* (Moscow, 1939).

Mochul'sky, K., "Klassitsizm v sovremennoi russkoi poezii," *Sovremennyya Zapiski*, XI (1922).

—— "O. E. Mandel'shtam," *Vstrecha*, November 1945.

—— "Poeticheskoye tvorchestvo Anny Akmatovoi," *Russkaya Mysl'*, March-April 1921.

Nedobrovo, N. V., "Anna Akhmatova," *Russkaya Mysl'*, July 1915.

Oksyonov, Innokenty, "Sovetskaya poeziya i nasledie akmeizma," *Literaturny Leningrad*, 1934, No. 24.

Oktyabr', 1946, No. 9.

Pertsov, V. "Chitaya Akhmatovu," *Literaturnaya Gazeta*, July 10, 1940, No. 38 (889).

Petrogradskaya Pravda, September 1, 1921.

Posluzhnoi Spisok Praporshchika 5 Gusarskago Aleksandriyskago Yeya Velichestva Gosudaryni Imperatritsy Aleksandry Fyodorovny Polka Gumilyova.

Selivanovsky, A., *Ocherki po Istorii Russkoi Sovetskoi Poezii* (Moscow, 1936).

Shelley, Gerald, tr., *Modern Poems from Russia* (London, 1942).

Stepanov, Nikolai, "Poeticheskoe nasledie akmeizma," *Literaturny Leningrad*, 1934, No. 35.

Strakhovsky, Leonid I., "Anna Akhmatova: The Sappho of Russia," *The Russian Student*, VI (1929), No. 3.

Struve, Gleb, "Blok and Gumilyov," *The Slavonic and East European Review*, XXV (November 1946), No. 64.

—— "Materialy dlya biografii N. S. Gumilyova. Po neizdannym dokumentam," *Novoye Russkoye Slovo*, December 16, 1947.

—— "Neizdannye stikhi N. Gumilyova," *Novy Zhurnal*, No. 8, 1944.

—— "Pis'ma o russkoi poezii," *Russkaya Mysl'*, 1922, Nos. 6-7.

—— "Tri sud'by: Blok, Gumilyov, Sologub," *Novy Zhurnal*, Nos. 16, 17, 1948.

Struve, Mikhail, "N. S. Gumilyovu," *Russkaya Mysl'*, 1921, Nos. 10-12.

Struve, Pyotr, "In Memoriam," *Russkaya Mysl'*, 1921, Nos. 10-12.

Svyatopolk-Mirsky, Kn. D., "O. Mandel'shtam: 'Shum Vremeni,'" *Sovremennyya Zapiski*, XXV (1925).

Terapiano, Yuri, "Poetika Gumilyova", *Novoye Russkoye Slovo*, July 20, 1947.

Tolstoy, A., "O literature i voine," *Literatura i Iskusstvo*, December 5, 1942, No. 49.

Tsekhnovitser, Orest, *Literatura i Mirovaya Voina* (Moscow, 1938).

Tsekh Poetov, Vols. I, II-III (Petersburg-Berlin).

Tumpovskaya, M., "'Kolchan' N. Gumilyova," *Apollon*, 1917, Nos. 6-7.

Vladislavlev, I. V., *Literatura Velikogo Desyatiletiya*, vol. I (Moscow-Leningrad, 1928).

Volkov, A., *Poeziya Russkogo Imperializma* (Moscow, 1935).

Zhirmunsky, V., "Preodolevshie simvolism," *Russkaya Mysl'*, 1916, No. 12.

Znamya, 1946, No. 10.